Bulwark of the Old Regime:
France's Royal Swedish Regiment in the French and American Revolutions

Neil Kent
Clément Chevalier

Bulwark of the Old Regime:
France's Royal Swedish Regiment in the French and American Revolutions

Neil Kent
Clément Chevalier

Academica Press
Washington~London

Library of Congress Cataloging-in-Publication Data

Names: Kent, Neil (author) | Chevalier, Clément (author)
Title: Bulwark of the old regime : france's royal swedish regiment in the french and american revolutions | Neil Kent and Clément Chevalier
Description: Washington : Academica Press, 2023. | Includes references.
Identifiers: LCCN 2023930191 | ISBN 9781680538502 (hardcover) | 9781680538519 (paperback) | 9781680538526 (e-book)

Copyright 2023 Neil Kent and Clément Chevalier

Bretagne, Lyonnais, immortal Legions.
And you, brave Germans, who from the icy lands of the North
Leaving your sovereigns without being unfaithful to them,
Come, under our flags, to give, to brave death.

**- Le Michaud d'Arçon, Jean,
"Ode sur la prise du Fort Saint-Philippe,"** *Histoire du siège de Gibraltar*

Contents

Introduction 1

Chapter 1:
Swedish Forces Change Sides 5
The Nine Years War 5
The Battle of Fleurus 5

Chapter 2:
Initial campaigns abroad 9
Military Action in Catalonia 9
Siege of Barcelona 12
The Treaty of Ryswick 13

Chapter 3:
The wars of succession 15
War of the Spanish Succession (1701-1714) 15
The Battle of Blenheim and its Consequences 17
The War of the Polish Succession 27
The War of the Austrian Succession 29

Chapter 4:
The first global wars 39
The Seven Years War 1756-63 39
The Treaty of Paris 44

Chapter 5:
The American Revolution and its Consequences 67
The American Revolution (1775-83) 67
Axel Fersen in America 70

First Phase of the French-American Join Military Engagement...................76

Second Phase of the Joint French-American Military Engagement.............77

Third Phase of the French-American Engagement..79

Swedish Officers in the American Revolution 87

The Sieges of Gibraltar (1779-83) and Minorca (1781-82).........................90

The Surrender of Minorca (1782)..92

Further campaigns of the Royal Swedish Regiment...................................101

Chapter 6:
The French Revolution and
the End of the Royal Swedish Regiment..105

Revolutionary Disturbances Commence 105

Fersen and the Flight of the Royal Family to Varennes 105

The end of the Royal Swedish Regiment...107

Index 111

Introduction

During the second half of the seventeenth century, Sweden was at the pinnacle of its territorial expanse and military power. Much of its success was due to its king, Gustav II Adolf (1594-1634), "the Lion of the North," who himself had fallen at the otherwise victorious Battle of Lützen, during the Thirty Years War (1618-48). Often perceived as a war between the Catholic and Protestant states of Europe, it was, in reality, more of a dynastic confrontation between two Catholic powers: the Bourbon monarchy of France, and its ally Sweden, against Habsburg Austria and its allies within the Holy Roman Empire. Although it was in relative terms the most devastating war Europe ever experienced, at its conclusion Sweden had greatly increase in size, influence and, prestige.

A variety of research has been carried out on France's Royal Swedish regiment, which played a major role under the *ancien régime*. Most studies are based on the memoirs of those who served in it and the impressions made on their contemporaries, peers, and families. Tactical treatises, so copious during this period, when military technology and tactics were constantly modified and improved, are also important sources. The Seven Years War (1756-63), in which the regiment played an important part, was arguably the world's first global war, with conflict taking place across the world. So, too, was the role of the Chevalier Jean Le Michaud d'Arçon, a military engineer who was tasked with devising an attack on the British fortifications at Gibraltar. As he would later opine:

> Our writers seem too little educated about our military constitution and the history of our troops. Why have none of them yet undertaken to write it? Our regiments are well worth the Sacred Battalion of the Thebans, and the Macedonian Phalanx, whose exaggerated exploits constantly tire our ears. Why has poetry not yet devoted its accents to the deserved praise of the defenders of the Fatherland? Chevert and d'Assas were as brave as Cynegirus and Regulus. Why do we only ever speak of the Ancients with ridiculous enthusiasm, and leave in oblivion those of the

Moderns who have honored their country or who have died in its defense?[1]

Sweden, a country in which Lutheranism was the established religion and the practice of Catholicism outside of embassies a capital crime, was, nonetheless, France's closest ally from the Thirty Years War until the French Revolution. With the defeat of King Charles XII, the warrior king, in his wars against Russia's emperor Peter the Great, Sweden's role as a great military power came to an end. The Treaty of Nystad, which ended hostilities on September 10, 1721, gave proof of this fact. Russian troops departed from occupied Finland, while Sweden transferred Estonia, Livonia, Ingria, Kexholm, and the Karelian Isthmus to Russia, receiving in exchange some two million silver thalers.

As the French monarchist politician, essayist, poet, and philosopher Viscount Louis Gabriel Ambroise de Bonald put it:

> The Swedes, allies of France, had the most disciplined army in Germany that had ever existed since Caesar's legions. They were almost always sure, says one author of the time, either to defeat those who opposed their valor, or to make perish with their patience those who would avoid combat. They waged war in all seasons of the year, and they subsisted for three months in quarters where the Imperial Army could not have lived for eight days. This was a result of the professional improvements and regulations brought in by King Gustav Adolf during the Thirty Years War, making it the Western world's most efficient army of its time.[2]

With the conclusion of the Thirty Years War, France's military and political influence in Europe had reached new heights. Furthermore, its relationship with Protestant Sweden had furthered its interests by giving it an ally within the politically weak Holy Roman Empire, since Sweden now had territory within it. Ultimately, France was able to expand at the expense of the German states, in part, because of this. The Viscount de Bonald had much praise for Sweden's fighting forces:

> The brave Swedes who had been the honor of their country and the terror of Germany, born in war, raised in war, raised for war, perished in war,

---

[1] Jean Le Michaud d'Arçon, "Ode sur la prise du Fort Saint-Philippe," *Histoire du siège de Gibraltar* (Paris, 1783), p. 104

[2] Louis Gabriel Ambroise de Bonald, *Législation primitive, considérée dans les derniers temps par les seules lumières de la raison*, Vol. 3 (Paris, 1802).

and very few saw their homeland again. The remnants of these valiant troops passed into the service of France, where their name and spirit were perpetuated in the two regiments of Royal-Suédois and Royal-Allemand.[3]

Yet the reality was somewhat different. During the Thirty Years War and after, most fighting men in the Royal Swedish Regiment were not Swedes, but mercenaries from all over Europe. The age of conscription and patriotism had not yet come.

From the time of the reign of King Louis XIV (1643-1715), nearly one-third of the French military consisted of foreigners. This was not unusual at the time, since the military forces of all states employed large components of mercenaries. Arguably the most important were the Swiss Guards, who were the personal bodyguards of the King of France up to the end of old regime in 1792. Accustomed to the rigors of the mountains, they were famed throughout Europe for their courage, discipline, and ferocity. Even today, they still guard the Pope. Also important was the German Brigade, which at first only included a regiment from Alsace but later included the Swedish Regiment. After the conclusion of the Thirty Years War, Sweden's territories in Germany, that is, within the Holy Roman Empire, included, Swedish Pomerania (1630-1815), Bremen and Verden (1648-1719), and Wismar (1648-1903, albeit leased to Mecklenburg from 1803). There was also a British contingent after the Glorious Revolution which saw King James II flee to France, in 1688, and which included both Irish and Scottish guardsmen who had gone into exile in the so-called "flight of the wild geese" as it was colloquially known. From 1671, there was a Royal Italian Regiment and from 1739, a Royal Corsican one as well. Finally, there was a regiment of light cavalry, the Hussars, established in 1692, which was increasingly composed of men who had fled Hungary during the revolt of Francis Rakoczi, Prince of Transylvania, against the Austrians, which last from 1703 to 1711. Highly valued for not only their abilities but their cost effectiveness, Étienne-François, Duc de Choiseul famously quipped that "the acquisition of one foreign soldier was

---

[3] Ibid.

equivalent to three men: one who was bought, one who was prevented from being bought by the enemy, and one kept for agriculture."[4]

Some of these men were deserters from other armies, while some were simply volunteers seeking work, often from smaller states on the periphery of Austrian or Prussian territories. The higher officers of these regiments tended to be German or Sweden, but the lower ones were often Alsatian. Loyalty among the ordinary soldiery was limited and desertion was frequent. As an old ditty of the *ancien régime* put it:

> My father is a Soldier of the King
> My mother is a foreigner
> Give me the King's penny
> So I can win over the baker.

---

[4] Quoted in Eugène Fieffé, *Histoire des troupes étrangères au service de la France: depuis leur origine jusqu'à nos jours*, Vol.1 (Paris, 1991, 1st ed. 1854).

Chapter 1:
Swedish Forces Change Sides

The Nine Years War

In the wake of his partially successful Dutch War (1672-1678), King Louis XIV's objective was to consolidate France's northwestern border against the Holy Roman Emperor Leopold I. As a preliminary measure, he occupied the Archbishopric of Cologne. He also sought to secure the French state internally and in 1685 revoked the Edict of Nantes, which in the previous century had granted religious toleration to Protestants. A pan-European alliance known as the League of Augsburg, formed by the Netherlands, England and Scotland, the Holy Roman Empire, the Duchy of Savoy, Portugal, Spain, and finally Sweden, stood in opposition to the king's vision.

Sweden, a staunch ally of France in the Dutch War, now deployed to the United Provinces an auxiliary corps consisting of six regiments of infantry. The first regiment was commanded by Count Adam Ludwig Lewenhaupt and set forth from Sweden. The five other regiments marched from Swedish Pomerania. The combined forces arrived in December 1688, forming a total of twelve companies, each made up of seventy men commanded by twelve officers, along with trumpeters and drummers. Their arrival coincided with the beginning of the Nine Years War, which lasted from 1688 to 1697.

The Battle of Fleurus

On July 1, 1690, the Battle of Fleurus, in southern Belgium, was fought by the League of Augsburg (England, Holland, Austria, Spain and Sweden) against France. It was a major engagement of the Nine Years War, though the conflict became global conflict and was fought in the

American colonies and along the African coast as well as in Europe. The main goal of the League of Augsburg was to restrict French expansion in Europe, particularly in the strategically and commercially important Netherlands.[5]

Two Swedish regiments, each containing 876 soldiers, took part. They were commanded by Count Nils Bielke and Baron Carl-Gustaf Erskine. There were also four companies belonging to the regiment of Gustaf Mauritanian Lewenhaupt, under the command of a Lieutenant-Colonel Sparfelt. The battle was a disaster for the Augsburg League, which sustained 50 percent casualties, including some five thousand prisoners. Following the customs of the time, these prisoners of war were offered the opportunity to change sides and fight for the French. To this end, King Louis XIV of France commanded Captain Johan Henrik Leisler, of his Swiss Stuppa-Jeune Regiment, to establish a new infantry formation, divided into ten companies comprising six hundred men in total. About one-sixth of them were Swedish subjects. Frans von Knorring, scion of a Finnish-Swedish noble family, was appointed its colonel.[6]

In a subsequent action the French, under the Marshal de Luxembourg, engaged the forces of the League of Augsburg and triumphed over those of the Prince von Waldeck. Nine thousand prisoners were taken, along with fifty-five canons and more than a hundred flags. Amongst those defeated were three companies of Lewenhaupt's regiment, whilst his others formed a garrison at Mons. These included two of the Pomeranian regiments: von Bielke's and Erskine's. At the battle's end, five hundred men of the Swedish auxiliary corps became prisoners, one of them from Lewenhaupt's Regiment, that is, two-thirds of the Swedes committed. In celebration of this victory, a *Te Deum* was sung at the Cathedral of Notre-Dame de Paris.

On July 25, 1690, the Alsatian Henri Leisler, a native of Berne and captain of the Swiss Infantry Regiment Stuppa-Jeune, incorporated the prisoners into the French armies. Leisler had seen active duty in Sicily, before participating at the Battle of Fleurus. By August the Regiment de

---

[5] Margareta Beckmann, *Under fransk fana! Royal Suédois. Svenskt Regemente i Fransk Tjänst. 1690-1791* (Stockholm, 1995), p. 9.
[6] Ibid., 11.

Leisler was incorporated into the French military as a "German" infantry regiment. Ten companies were established, totaling five hundred men who had previously fought in the United Provinces as the Swedish regiment. Its officers were Swedish, to which Leisler added some of his own comrades from the Infantry Stuppa-Jeune.[7]

---

[7] Comte F. U. Wrangel, *Origines et débuts du royal-Suédois actuellement 89e de ligne* (Paris, 1914).

Chapter 2:
Initial campaigns abroad

Military Action in Catalonia

The following year, 1691, an additional twelve companies were incorporated into the Regiment de Leisler, adding another 600 men. The enlarged unit joined the French army at the southern border, under command of the Duc de Noailles. Its first engagement, in July 1691, was in Spanish Catalonia. It also assisted in the Siege of Urgel. In April 1693, it participated in the Siege of Rosas, led by the Swedish officers Frans von Knorring, Åke Ulfsparre, Bernt Wilhelm Taube, and a Captain Franck. All survived, but after the successful Siege of Hostalric, in July 1694, Leisler died of the wounds suffered in the assault.[8]

Far from northern Europe, there was little chance that the Swedes would face their compatriots in combat. Other major difficulties confronted them, however, particularly the difficult terrain. The Panissars Pass, for example, "was so narrow that one had to arrive two by two at the front."[9]

Meanwhile, in the north, the Battle of Leuze-en-Hainaut took place in what is today Belgium on 18 September 1691. The victorious Marshal de Luxembourg defeated the Prince of Orange. This success was repeated in a rematch the following year at the Battle of Steenkerque.

The fresh theater of war in Catalonia, where the new Swedish regiment was fighting, proved less promising. Although the Swedes engaged in military action in Catalonia in 1693, payment was not forthcoming. As the young officer Åke Ulfsparre wrote:

---

[8] Beckmann, p. 12.
[9] Erik-Gustave Geyer, citing Ulfsparre Åke, "Lettres," in *Histoire de Suède depuis les premiers temps jusqu'à nos jours* (1801) (Brussels, 1845).

> There is more misery here than one can imagine, as the soldiers have not been paid for several months. The soldiers are happier than the officers. If we don't get paid soon, I fear we shall all be forced to leave the service, and many of us are already resigned to it.[10]

Some men left the regiment in disgust. Those who remained took part in the Siege of Rosas, in Catalonia, from June 1 to 13, 1692. This was the first official engagement of the Swedish Regiment.

A few weeks later, on July 29, the Marshal de Luxembourg triumphed again at the Battle of Neerwinden, supported by Patrick Sarsfield, the 1st Earl of Lucan, a devoted supporter of the exiled Catholic branch of the House of Stuart. It was the bloodiest battle of the seventeenth century and Lord Lucan fell, but the French forces held out. William of Orange himself was heard to mutter, "Oh! Insolent Nation!"[11] In the battle's aftermath, he further expounded, "Is it possible that I will never beat that hunchback?" To which, Luxembourg acidly remarked, on hearing about it, "How does he know that I am a hunchback? He has never seen me from behind."[12]

Luxembourg more proudly wrote King Louis XIV:

> Your enemies have done wonders, your troops even better. The Princes of your blood have surpassed themselves. As for me, Sire, I have no other merit than to have carried out your orders. You told me to attack a city and fight a battle; I took one and won the other.[13]

The triumph in Paris was complete. So many flags were taken from the enemy at Neerwinden and placed in the arches of the Notre-Dame that Luxembourg became known as "the upholsterer" of the Cathedral.[14]

In 1694, King Louis XIV reopened the front in Catalonia. His démarche began with a major false step. Noailles's Expeditionary Corps attempted to take Gérone, while passing the River Ter, which was guarded by Spanish forces. The French forces were overwhelmed: three thousand men of the Expeditionary Corps were killed, while sixteen flags were taken, along with a large quantity of equipment. Nevertheless, from June

---

[10] Ibid.
[11] Marquis de Ségur, *Le tapissier de Notre-Dame, les dernières années du maréchal de Luxembourg, 1678-1695* (Paris, 1907), p. 568.
[12] Ibid., 568.
[13] Ibid., 568.
[14] Ibid., 568.

6 to 10, Palamos fell to battalions of French, German, Swiss, and Irish troops. This was followed by another siege of Gérone and a French advancement toward Barcelona, the Catalonian capital. Noailles's forces besieged Hostalric on July 12 and captured it a week later. Leisler was killed there, however, lowering morale alongside lack of payment.

In September, Noailles captured Castelfollit and then took his troops into winter quarters while being harassed by enemy forces, leaving him to lament that, 'The enemies are more wicked this winter than usual."[15] Both Taube and von Knorring each commanded companies in the action, but command of the regiment was not filled after Leisler's death. The officers were keen for the regiment to rejoin the main theater of combat, in the north-east of France. Ulfsparre wrote, "Since I would then be closer to Sweden and to the place where the regiment is at the moment, I would have an easier time learning everything about the war." Von Knorring himself fell during this period, but there was a gold, if not silver lining to this sad event, since, as Ulfsparre put it, "He has left to his widow, as a consolation, a great quantity of *Louis d'or.*"[16]

On October 20, 1694, Erik Magnus Sparre, Major von Fürstenberg, Count of Sunday and Baron de Sparre (1665-1726), was named colonel of the Swedish Regiment, a post he took up at Perpignan on April 13, 1695. He had participated in all of its campaigns since 1688 and combined both military and diplomatic skills in his person. This event, "was very pleasant for us Swedes." In consequence, the regiment now assumed the appellation Sparre's Regiment.

In 1695, the French forces attempted to strengthen their front in Catalonia, which proved difficult to accomplish. Noailles had fallen sick, so the troops were now commanded by the Duke de Vendôme, a great-grandson of King Henry IV and his mistress Gabrielle d'Estrée, who had helped convince him to convert to Roman Catholicism to gain the throne. Vendômee impressed Ulfsparre, who described him as, "fearless, gentle, and well meaning; he knows neither hate, nor envy, nor vengeance." Others, however, considered him crude, lazy, insouciant, and debauched. He was also criticized for neglecting not only the details of administration

---

[15] Geyer
[16] Ibid.

but also his own personal hygiene. Despite his illegitimate birth, he was immensely proud of his royal ancestry as a prince of the blood. Still, he was a true warrior and father of his troops. "In war, he has unparalleled courage, alertness and presence of mind." Fully aware of his value in this regard, he declared, after he was informed that his services had been fully paid up, "You have made a mistake, men like me are only ultimately paid in words and scrolls."[17]

Despite Vendôme's bravado, from March to August 1695 his forces were held in check in Catalonia by other foreign troops allied with Spain, specifically those commanded by Prince George of Hesse-Darmstadt, a cousin of the Spanish queen. When they were blocked at Castellfollit and later at Palamos, Sparre was injured. By the dawn of 1696, a stalemate ensued and a temporary calm reigned. Erik Sparre used the occasion to reorganize his regiment. Three of his own nephews joined, including Karl Magnus Toffeta, Baron de Sparre (d. 1754), as well his second-cousin, Second Lieutenant Lars Magnus Sparre (1664-1725).

On June 1, 1696, Vendôme was victorious, finally defeating Hesse-Darmstadt at Hostalric. Hostilities ceased on August 29 with the Treaty of Turin, which put an end to the regional military ambitions of Victor-Amadeus, Duke of Savoy. With the advent of peace, the Swedish Regiment's role in serving France seemed bleak and almost all Swedes departed. As Åke Ulfsparre put it, "at the moment any Swedes in the regiment other than the gentleman Oxhufvud, captain of the infantry."[18]

Siege of Barcelona

Peace did not reign for long in Catalonia. French forces besieged Barcelona, the Catalonian capital, from 15 June to 8 August 1697. Some 15,000 bombs and 100,000 cannon balls rained down upon the city.[19] The siege was difficult, for a sea blockade was impossible to secure. Enemy forces also used firearms with a new firing mechanism, the Miquelet lock, which enabled gunpowder to be ignited in wet and windy weather. Among those who fell were Second Lieutenants Axel Sparre Gabrielson, Erik

---

[17] Ibid.
[18] Ibid.
[19] Beckmann, p. 15.

Hård, and a member of the Bonde family.[20] By the time Barcelona capitulated in August 1697, casualties totaled eighteen officers and some three hundred men. Soon after they retired into winter quarters in Roussillon and were reduced to six companies, their wages suffering a similar fate.[21]

At the Battle of Hospitalet, the Duke de Vendôme was again victorious, this time against José Fernández de Velasco, 8th Duke of Frías (ca. 1665-1704). The cost was high for the French, with no fewer than 10,000 killed and wounded, including 160 captains and 322 lieutenants. Another 160 men were also taken prisoner. The Swedish Regiment suffered eighteen fatal casualties among the officers. Count Sparre lamented, "My regiment has suffered greatly, I have had 18 officers killed or wounded and close to 300 soldiers. One could also say that our new Swedes who were keen to see and assist in some dazzling military actions have been contented and I am very impressed by their conduct."[22]

In the wake of this action, the companies of Taube and Knorring were reformed. Taube had fallen in 1694, but had noted that he had had enough, not of battle but of French bureaucratic failings.[23] Sparre had fathered a child, who was raised by a local priest and eventually also joined the regiment. By then, Sparre was ambassador in Paris. This benefited the young second lieutenant, who received a pension of 2,000 livres a year, deducted from the latter's own French pension of 12,000 livres, on condition of making nor further claims on his father's estate in Sweden.[24]

The Treaty of Ryswick

The Treaty of Ryswick concluded the Nine Years' War. Many benefits accrued to France's enemies. Louis XIV accepted the accession to the English throne of the Protestant King William III and Queen Mary, daughter of the ousted Catholic King James II. They also regained conquered territories. France also reaped benefits from the treaty. Various

---

[20] Ibid., 16.
[21] Ibid., 16.
[22] Gunnar Lindbergh, *Un colonel du Royal-Suédois, le Comte Erik Sparre (1665-1726)* (Paris, 1939).
[23] Ibid.
[24] Ibid., 17.

commercial accords were settled to France's benefit, including Spain's cession of Santo Domingo and Tortuga to France. The former, renamed Saint-Domingue, would soon become France's most important colony, with hundreds of thousands of slaves toiling on its prosperous plantations. In celebration the French composer Jean Gilles commemorated the event with a *Te Deum* in the city of Toulouse, as did Sébastien de Brossard, with his *Grand Motet Canticum Aucharisticum Pro Pace*, which was sung in the Chapel Royal. On 25 March, France, England, and the Netherlands agreed to the new territorial arrangements. Another *Te Deum* was sung in honor of the peace, composed by Nicolas Bernier.

Dark clouds already loomed on the horizon. They had been gathering for decades, as far back as 1665, when the ill health of King Charles II of Spain and inability to produce male heirs raised the issue of who would succeed him. This matter came to a head upon his death in 1700. On the one hand, there was Louis XIV, whose consort Maria-Theresa of Austria was a daughter of King Philip IV of Spain and half-sister to Charles. Since Spain did not bar women from succeeding, Louis XIV's son, the Dauphin Louis, was a prime candidate. On the other hand, the Holy Roman Emperor Leopold I, uncle of Charles II, laid a Habsburg claim. Pope Innocent XII decided in favor of France, but with the caveat that since the dauphin was already expected to inherit the French throne and pass it on to his first-born son and his heirs, Spain would go to his second son, Philip, Duke of Anjou. The expiring Charles II accepted this arrangement. He died on 1 November 1700, and on 16 November Louis XIV proclaimed his grandson, Philip of Anjou King Philp V of Spain. With Spain brought under the Bourbons, the Spanish ambassador to France proclaimed, "the Pyrenees no longer exist." In one fell swoop, the balance of European power was upset to the horror of more than just the Habsburgs. England was loath to see its historic enemy France strengthened to such a degree and feared for its security.

Chapter 3:
The wars of succession

War of the Spanish Succession (1701-1714)

With Philip's ascension to the throne of Spain, the stage was set for a new European conflagration. Louis XIV also sought to secure a rapprochement with Savoy through his grandson's marriage to its dynastic house. France's perennial enemies, Austria, England, Prussia, Portugal, and Aragon, as well as its internal ones – the rebellious Huguenots Camisards, who lived in the mountainous Cévennes and Vaunage regions in the south of France – refused to accept this aggrandizement. Arrayed with France against them were the electorates of Cologne and Bavaria, as well as the duchies of Mantua and Savoy. In the face of impending hostilities, the Royal Swedish Regiment was enlarged by two battalions and sent northwards under the joint command of Louis, Duke of Burgundy (1682–1712), brother of Philip, and Louis-François, Duke de Boufflers and Marshal of France (1644-1711). Its role at this stage remained defensive.

A *casus belli* soon obtruded. With the death of King James II in exile on 16 September 1701, France declared its support for his Catholic son, the "Old Pretender," to assume the thrones of England, Scotland, and Ireland as King James III. That same year, the Swedish Regiment was transferred to the Spanish Netherlands, where it joined other French forces in anticipation of a war between France, on the one hand, and Austria, England, and the Netherlands on the other. Fighting finally broke out on 15 May 1702, when France's three main antagonists declared war. The Swedish Regiment departed for Flanders. The first battle of this War of the Spanish Succession took place at Nijmegen, in western Holland, on 11 June. The joint forces of the Duke of Burgundy were victorious. The

Swedish officer Louis Sparre, in particular, distinguished himself for valor in the battle. The action then moved to the German front.

Battle ensued at Hulst in August and at Ruremonde and Andernach in September, both French victories. The following year, Eckeren was also conquered. Shortly thereafter, Sweden's warrior king Karl XII (reigned 1697-1718) needed reinforcements for military action in Poland, in the long, drawn-out conflict that came to be known as the Great Northern War, and eventually included Russia (1700-21) as Sweden's major enemy. The war would prove disastrous for Sweden. Karl soon lost ground to Peter the Great (reigned 1682-1725) and was forced to cede Swedish Ingria to the tsar, a territory on which Peter's new capital of St. Petersburg arose. Sparre absented himself from Holland to serve his king in the east, participating in the Siege of Thorn, which took place from May to September 1703. Injured, he returned to France that November. The following year, promoted by Louis XIV to major-general, he led his regiment into the Rhineland.

On 30 August 1702, Claude-Louis-Hector de Villars, Marshal of France, took some of the French forces on the Rhine to the territory of France's ally Bavaria. A splendid tactician and strategist, he was greatly valued by Louis XIV and put his king's interest above his own. A courtier famously commented to the king, "Marshal de Villars does his business very well," to which the monarch responded, "Yes, but he does my business well, too."[25] Later, Villars would describe the battles of Malplaquet (1709) and Denain (1712) to Voltaire while he was writing his famed *Century of Louis XIV*, published in 1751.

On 28 September, the Holy Roman Empire declared war on France. By December, the Royal Swedish Regiment had taken up winter quarters at Tournai, which France had annexed in 1668. King Philip's prospective marriage to a member of the Savoyard royal house came to naught, and on 5 January 1703 Savoy transferred its support to France's enemies, thereby creating another front.

In view of these threats, Louis XIV commissioned Baron Nathanael de Hook, an officer of the English Royal Guards, to reform the Swedish Regiment. De Hook served in this capacity until 1710. Alongside other

---

[25] Fadi El Hage, *Le maréchal de Villars, l'infatigable Bonheur* (Paris, 2012), p. 192.

changes at the top, Sparre converted to Roman Catholicism in the presence of the Bishop of Tournai, and also married a French lady of his new faith, the daughter of Joseph Alexandre Le Vaillant de la Bassardrie. Sparre's conversion was no small act, for it had immense legal consequences in Sweden. A sixteenth-century law made conversion to Catholicism a capital crime without appeal. Sparre's property was confiscated and he was technically forbidden to return to his country. Yet Sweden was France's closest ally, so Charles XII awarded Sparre an annual pension of 3,000 livres. Sparre's participation in the Battle of Ekeren, on 30 June, demonstrated that neither the French nor the Swedish king would be disappointed in him. With two of his fellow Swedish officers, Kibling and Andrews, wounded, he was rewarded with promotion to the rank of Field Marshal. The following year, 1704, the Swedish Regiment was transferred to the Moselle region but engaged in no military action there. De Villars, meanwhile, was transferred to the fractious Cévennes.

The Battle of Blenheim and its Consequences

The Battle of Blenheim, on 13 August 1704, was a decisive defeat for the French by John Churchill, Duke of Marlborough. The campaign continued, however, and in October 1705 the regiment participated in the Battle of Ballar. The following year it resumed campaigning in Flanders, where, together with the rest of the French forces, it was again defeated by the intrepid English duke. In early 1705, Villars returned from the Cévennes, where he had campaigned against the Camisards, and led his troops in anticipation of a new attack by Marlborough. Villars was thorough, and he visited the entire front, "without neglecting a ravine, a clump of trees, a stream, a mound, a powder keg. He is preoccupied with the morale of the troops, the reform of abuses, the strengthening of discipline." There are complaints about the lack of officers: "There are entire regiments commanded by one lieutenant."[26] He encouraged his men to labor only on the entrenchments they were constructing to the degree that they were useful. In consequence, he raised morale and strengthened

---

[26] Ibid., 192.

his troops' effectiveness. "They have never been so beautiful, never so full of ardor," he wrote

> I dare to say that I follow and practice that which can inspire and conserve this ardor. The soldiers hold good speeches, which they consider far better than those of their enemies. Such is the spirit in the army and with respect to desertion, which is quite a problem amongst our enemies, very little, since our troops are well-paid, well provided with bread and meat, the soldiers cheerful.[27]

In these positive circumstances, Marlborough finally appeared before Villars, at Sierck, in June 1705. Villars's forces, including the Royal Swedish Regiment, numbered some 55,000 men. Marlborough's forces numbered 90,000, but awaited the arrival of 30,000 reinforcements from Baden. His men, in contrast with those of the French and their allies, were decimated by desertions. Some question his military probity as well. In any case, to avoid a disaster, Marlborough retreated to Trier, to the stupefaction of most of Europe, which was eagerly awaiting news of the confrontation. Villars responded with disdain: "He believes he has swallowed me like a grain of salt."[28] In fact, the relationship between the two men had a cordiality hard to imagine between enemies on the field in our own day. Before his retreat, Marlborough had sent Villars a strawberry liqueur, wine from Palma, and cider. After he withdrew, Marlborough sent a polite message saying that he had done so only with great regret and for reasons over which he had no control.

Serving with Villars, the Swedish Regiment entered the Rhineland. An inventory made on 17 October confirms four lieutenant-colonels, of whom two were Swedish, La Gardie and Lenck. It also included Major Sparre. There were also ten captains, five of whom were Swedish. Of a further fifteen captains, seven were Swedes. There were also twelve ensigns, five of them Swedish.

High morale among both officers and men would be tested in 1706. The regiment was sent early that year to join the Army of Flanders, now under the command of Marshal de Villeroy, of whom it was said "he was

---

[27] "La dernière campagne de Villars," *Revue historique de l'Armée, publication trimestrielle de l'État-Major de l'Armée*, No. 1, July 1945.
[28] Ibid.

no more than an old wrinkled balloon, from which all the air that had inflated it had escaped."[29] On 23 May 1706, the French forces were routed at Ramillies, in the province of Brabant. The Bavarian forces lost their foothold, and the Swedes covered the French retreat. They then reinforced the garrison at Ménin. An English officer noted, "It was a truly distressing sight to see the sad remains of this mighty army reduced to a handful."[30] Villeroy, losing his composure in the face of this debacle, had simply given up in Flanders. He had not even been with his troops there, having instead positioned himself in Alsace, where he constructed a defensive line along the River Lauter. When he heard of the debacle in Flanders, he exclaimed, "the French defeat at Ramillies is the most shameful, the most humiliating, and the most disastrous of defeats."[31] Ménin was besieged from 22 July to 20 August, when the French garrison capitulated. The Swedish Lieutenant-Colonel Gooke and Captain Stützer were praised for their valor. One of the regiment's officers fell, with another five wounded. Of the enlisted men, fifty were killed and 106 wounded. This was only a small part of the debacle, but Villeroy's reputation was ruined and he was ostracized by the king. Only in 1712 was he partly reprieved through the intervention of Madame de Maintenon, the king's *maîtresse-en-titre*. When Louis died in 1715, it was he who delivered the codicil of the king's last will and testament enabling Philip of Orleans to become Regent of France after the monarch's death.

Throughout 1707, Sparre's Swedish Regiment remained in Flanders, now under the Duc de Vendôme, who had returned from Italy to replace the disgraced Villeroy. They remained in a defensive position along a line running from Mons, Charleroi, and Namur, dotted with redoubts and demarcated by natural obstacles against any attacker. Maneuvers continued on both sides without direct confrontation.

Sparre returned to Sweden that year, leaving the regiment under the command of Jakob Gustaf Lenck (1660-1734), who had previously taken charge during his absences. Lenck commanded the regiment's troops in

---

[29] Louis de Rouvroy, duc de Saint-Simon, *Mémoires*, Vol. II, 1701-1707 (Paris, 1728), p. 1983.
[30] Corelli Barnett, *Marlborough*, (London, 1999), p. 288.
[31] "La dernière campagne de Villars."

the Battle of Oudenarde, in Flanders, on 11 July 1708, which France lost. The Swedes were, however, part of the French victory at the Battle of Douai, shortly before the Treaty of Utrecht ended hostilities in 1713. France lost various territories, but Philip V was confirmed on the Spanish throne.

In May 1707, Marshal de Villars, still based on the Rhine, assumed the role of diplomat after taking a part of the enemy line at Stollhofen. He proposed to take French forces into the German states to join up with the troops of France's ally, Sweden's warrior king, Karl XII. The latter was encamped in Saxony and prepared to declare war on the Holy Roman Emperor. Karl XII met up with the Swedes near Nuremberg. This action deeply alarmed the Duke of Marlborough, who left Haye and strove to block the Swedish monarch. He was rebuffed by Karl, however, who soon departed for Russia in order to wage war against Peter the Great, a campaign that ended with the disastrous defeat at Poltava. The Swedish Regiment retired to winter quarters.

In January 1708, the Duke of Burgundy, with the assistance of Vendôme, took command of the French Army of Flanders, which included the Royal Swedish Regiment. Their collaboration was unsuccessful. Vendôme and Sparre's personalities clashed. The former was haughty, grave, austere, and little given to experiment with tactics. The latter was more earthy and pragmatic, having passed through the crucible of battle many times.

In the early months of 1708, the Swedes saw no action, but were back in the fight by summer. On 8 July, the great Flemish cities of Ghent and Bruges were taken, though Oudenarde proved a defeat. This left the route to Paris open to the enemy, who, it was feared, now envisioned an invasion of France itself. Lille was also threatened, and de Boufflers rushed there with some 15,000 men. As the year drew on, one of the worst winters to hit Europe, the so-called Great Winter of 1709, undermined military action among all the participants. Everyone now preferred peace, in practice if not on paper, for Louis XIV would not accept the conditions offered by the allies. In January 1709, continuing bad weather blocked the king's efforts. The only significant event was the promotion of Lars Sparre to the rank of lieutenant-colonel, which enabled him to command a battalion of the RSR.

On 15 March, Villars, with the assistance of de Boufflers, took control of the Army of Flanders. Their primary concern was to reverse the army's pervasive defeatism: "the misery was extreme, no clothing, no boots, no weapons, no bread, no military stores, no food arriving ... Just imagine the horror of seeing an army without bread!"[32] Yet the military were not the only ones suffering at this time. Throughout France there was famine and bread was difficult to obtain. Nonetheless, Villars was able to carry out new recruitments, reinforce discipline and order, and convince noble officers to renounce their salaries to provide for others. By contrast, the Allies, still under the Duke of Marlborough, were well fed, well clothed, well paid, and well disciplined. It was, therefore, no surprise when the great commander took Tournai and besieged Mons, in July, with 120,000 men.

By August, however, the French were recouping their losses and sorting out their logistical problems. When the Battle of Malplaquet took place on 11 September 1709, spirits were again high and, in this deeply pious age, religious devotions were zealously performed. Villars wrote, "One hour before daybreak, I had a shave and a powder. Our chaplain said mass for us and after a short sermon we were granted a general absolution."[33] Soon after, the battle commenced, with French troops on the right wing in the Forest of Lanière.

At 8 a.m., the Swedish Regiment engaged the English Guards, when

> The King's Regiment ordered a discharge from a great distance which did not shake them. That of Charest where Sparre's regiment was took its own action which reversed the right of the English, where their Guards battalions were, which proceeded some 200 steps with their flags, but supported by the English brigade of Orrery, where the Duke of Argyll was, it returned to charge, and entered the fray at the same time that the rest of their lines into our entrenchment.[34]

---

[32] El Hage, *Le maréchal de Villars,* p. 192.
[33] "La dernière campagne de Villars."
[34] Chevalier de Quincy, *Mémoires,* Paris, 1898.

Meanwhile, the Dutch infantry attacked three lines of trenches situated to the right of the French line, under the command of Boufflers. The enemy, under the command of the young Prince of Orange, attacked three or four times and were chopped to pieces. To the left, the line was embedded in the Forest of Sars, and Villars stripped his central body of men in order to contain the breach. He also ordered his artillery to fire on the mass of the enemy, who were hurling themselves at the center of the line. His sword was broken in the fracas. Prince Eugène of Savoy then launched his cavalry against those of the French, who charged six times. The cavalry of the Prince of Hesse turned the French right, which fell back. Finally, however, Villars ordered Boufflers and Puységur to undertake a disciplined retreat.

With the battle becoming a murderous frontal confrontation, Villars decided to halt the advance while killing as many of the enemy as possible. These casualties were heavy enough to prevent them from continuing the campaign. According to witnesses at the time, Malplaquet "was altogether a type of infernal mouth, a chasm of fire, sulfur, and saltpeter, where it seems nothing can approach without perishing in the conflagration."[35] The courage of the French troops was noted at the time, that to the right of the battlefield, "the soldiers have not had bread for two days, and throw away the bread they are given in order to fight."[36] Altogether, the Allies suffered 20,000 casualties and the French 10,000. Five lieutenant-generals were killed. Villars wrote, "the enemy has taken three or four flags. I myself have 30 of theirs in my chamber and I am still being brought more."[37] Boufflers fell back to Maubeuge with Sparre. Villars was carried away to Le Quesnoy, where he was secretly offered the viaticum out of fear that he will soon be killed. He responded, "No, since the army could not see Villars dying bravely, it is good that it sees him die as a Christian."[38]

Malplaquet was a strategic defeat despite the imbalance in losses. Still, it was a success for the morale of the French and their allies. As Villars wrote to Louis XIV:

---

[35] "Panégyrique du prince Eugène," *Dictionnaire Larousse du XIXe siècle,* 1873.
[36] Ibid.
[37] "La dernière campagne de Villars."
[38] Ibid.

if God grants us the grace to lose another such battle, Your Majesty can count on his enemies being destroyed ... The series of misfortunes that has befallen Your Majesty's armies in these recent years had so humiliated the French nation that people hardly dared to call themselves French. However, I can assure you, Sire, that the name Frenchman has never evoked such esteem as it has done now among the Allied army.[39]

This was a grand sentiment from someone who did not always see eye-to-eye with the French monarch. Sparre's regiment had lost two captains, ten lieutenants, and a hundred enlisted men. Villars reproached the right flank of his army for not having aided the center when it was attacked. No opprobrium fell on him at court, however, and he was made a peer of France shortly thereafter.

By now, another powerful military leader was lining up with the Allies, Prince Maurice of Saxony. The Swedish Regiment was strengthened. Jakob Gustaf Lenck was promoted to lieutenant-colonel. Sparre, the proprietor and colonel of the regiment, edited a new *Military Code* for its conduct.

Throughout 1710, various proposals emerged to restore peace, but nothing was achieved. France won further victories in Spain, but the Swedes remained on garrison duty for the whole of this period. In 1711, further negotiations occurred, but the horizon now looked brighter for France, as England was becoming increasingly uneasy with its Austrian ally. The Holy Roman Emperor Charles VI seemed keen on restoring his domains to their fullest extent under Charles V. This posed a potential threat to English security. Combat broke out anew on 6 July over the Fortress of Arleux, which was taken and retaken at considerable cost to both sides. The Swedes were called into action again and performed well.

Politics in England now interfered. The Duke of Marlborough fell into disgrace and was relieved of command, to be replaced by the Duke of Ormond, who favored peace and oversaw only stalemate in the field. Negotiations resumed at the Congress of Utrecht, which opened on 29 January 1712. Louis XIV's position had strengthened, but the allies were besieging various cities with little relief in sight. In consequence, the king ordered Villars to fall back from the Somme. Yet he remained belligerent

---

[39] Voltaire, *Le siècle de Louis XIV* (Paris, 2005), p. 59.

and demanded that his commander, "not follow the timid counsels to fall back to the Loire. He should go to fight at the head of his army and perish with it, if need be."[40]

On 24 July 1712, Villars achieved a great victory at Denain. He had put pressure on the wings of Prince Eugène's forces, which raised the siege of Landrecies. The Swedes played no role here, but did later participate in the recapture of Douai, Le Quesnoy, and Bouchain. With these successful operations, the Flemish Campaign came to an end.

The Great Northern War, in which Sweden fought Peter the Great's Russia, continued. Sweden won the Battle of Gadebusch, in which Prince Moritz of Saxony (Maurice de Saxe, 1696-1753) distinguished himself at the head of a Saxon regiment. He was the son of Frederick Augustus I, King of Poland and Elector of Saxony, who was the most powerful ruler in his corner of Europe. As the saying went, "When August has been drinking, Poland is drunk." He would serve under both Prince Eugène (Malplaquet) and under Field Marshal von der Schulenburg. He himself would become a field marshal in 1744. His reputation would be sullied by his illegitimate birth and from his conduct in the Duchy of Courland, in the northeastern Baltic, in 1726-1727. Although he called himself Duke of Courland, the Russians had sent him packing. Nonetheless, he was noted for his writings, which provided insight into the conduct of war and military tactics. They were based on what he called "My fantasies," a mixture of solid and serious thinking, actual hallucinations, bizarre concepts and mad epiphanies. A great womanizer, what gave him the greatest kudos was his success in making the future Empress Anna of Russia his mistress.[41]

Finally, from January to July 1713, peace negotiations ensued, leading to the Treaty of Utrecht. The allied rulers, with the exception of the Austrian Holy Roman Emperor, accepted that Louis XIV's grandson would retain his Spanish throne but would not be permitted to inherit that of the old French king after his death. Lacking a son of his own, Emperor Charles VI now promulgated his Pragmatic Sanction, which strove to assure the succession rights of his daughters to the various remaining

---

[40] El Hage, *Le maréchal de Villars*, p. 13.
[41] Jean-Pierre Bois, *Maurice de Saxe* (Fayard, 1992).

hereditary Habsburg territories, should there be no male heirs. This did not include the daughters of his elder brother Joseph I, who had reigned from 1705 to 1711. Nonetheless, the imperial dignity was not made hereditary but remained elective, even if the tradition for centuries was to award it to a Habsburg archduke.

As the war with the Holy Roman Empire continued, the RSR, under Marshall de Villars, retook Landau on 21 August, followed by Fribourg on 30 October. On 26 November, Villars met up with Prince Eugène at Rastatt, in order to negotiate a final peace with the Holy Roman Emperor. The Treaty of Rastatt, signed on 6 March 1714, finally concluded the war.

In consequence of the imminent peace, the RSR was reduced to only one battalion, composed of eight companies. In February 1714, Colonel de Sparre gave up his commission and retired to Sweden. On 10 March, with Sparre gone, Lieutenant Colonel Jakob Gustaf Lenck bought the RSR, adding the noble prefix 'de' to his surname, appropriate to his new military dignity. The uniform colors were changed to blue and red, with a yellow livery, while the flag now proclaimed, "Colonel and ordinance." With peace reigning in Western Europe for a generation, the RSR would not see battle there again for nineteen years.

The Great Northern War continued, however, and on 3 April 1715, King Karl XII of Sweden signed a treaty of alliance with France, a great boon. This was one of the last acts on the political stage of Louis XIV. He died from an anal fistula, complicated by gangrene, on 1 September. His great-grandson ascended the throne as King Louis XV (reigned 1715-1774), under the regency of Philippe, Duke of Orleans, which ended in 1723, when Louis reached his majority.

As for the RSR, its excellent relationship to the French crown continued and Charles Magnus Toffeta, Baron de Sparre, now became a colonel. Following this elevation, he saw to it that his eldest son, Joseph-Magnus de Toffeta, Baron of Kronberg and Count de Sparre, albeit only eleven years of age, entered the regiment. Since his wife's death in 1713, he had consigned his son to his brother-in-law, who was a canon of Tournai.

With the Spanish throne now secured for the Bourbons, Spain's new King Philip V attempted to restore Spain to its former glories, especially focusing on Italy and its numerous statelets. He also hoped that if Louis XV died without heirs, he himself might be the next in line to the French throne. France joined the Quadruple Alliance in 1717, which in 1718 declared war on Spain, irrespective of the fact that the monarchs of France and Spain were cousins. It also did not prevent Philip V from participating in the Conspiracy of Cellamare, a failed plot to remove Phillip of Orleans from his role as regent. In response to these events, France declared war on Spain on 9 January 1719. In May, the RSR was sent to Navarre under the command of Marshal de Berwick, who took Fontarabie and Saint-Sébastian.

The war continued into 1720. With new weapons technology increasing fire power and effectiveness, it became clear to all participants that new tactics were required. Order lines were thus abandoned in favor of more aggressive approaches allowing for greater mobility. The problem was that every military commander now had his own idea of what was optimum in the situations in which he found himself. The Marquis de Puységur, de Folard, and Guibert were those tacticians who now came to the fore, favoring chopped order lines, deep order lines, and mixed order lines, respectively. Puységur also advocated for increased mobility within the infantry, including attacks in columns rather than in strict line formations. Yet most of this remained theoretical. In any case, with military action very limited, the RSR regiment remained small in size, comprised of only seven hundred men. Lars Sparre returned to civil life in Paris, in very straitened financial circumstances. His son Joseph was elevated to the rank of lieutenant within the RSR, however. On 20 February 1720, The Hague Treaty ended the War of the Quadruple Alliance, after only modest military action.

On 7 August 1727, Charles de Sparre was named a brigadier of the infantry, and the regiment took part in training at La Sambre. Three years later, on 4 April 1730, Joseph Magnus de Toffeta de Sparre was elevated to the rank of captain. In 1732, the regiment moved to Alsace for further training.

The War of the Polish Succession

The War of the Polish Succession broke out in 1733. It erupted over the succession to the throne of Poland of Frederick Augustus II, who had succeeded his father as Elector of Saxony by hereditary right and hoped to secure election to replace him as Poland's monarch under the name Augustus III. France, Spain, and Sardinia instead favored the Polish magnate Stanisław Leszczyński, the father-in-law of King Louis XV. Russia, Austria, and Prussia supported Augustus. It was Cardinal Fleury, rather than the young Louis XV who declared war on the Habsburg Emperor Charles VI over the dispute.

The war began with a French invasion of Lorraine. Two armies were sent to Italy, under Villars, and also to the Rhineland, under Berwick. The RSR, with three battalions under Berwick's command, occupied Nancy and then Longwy. On 5 November, another company was formed for the RSR, by Captain Joseph de Toffeta de Sparre. Pierre Appelgrehn became a lieutenant-colonel in the regiment.

In early 1734, the RSR was placed under the command of Marshal de Belle-Isle, who took Trier and Trarback and laid siege to Philipsburg. Berwick, 63 years old, fell while leading his men in battle. He had mounted the trench while singing:

> Mr. Fickle, she says,
> is not for you, boy,
> but for a man of war,
> who has a beard on his chin
> and wears a feathered hat
> and boots with red heels.
>
> And the soldiers respond:
> Bellona will reduce to ashes
> the curtains of Phillipsbourg.
> with 80,000 Alexanders
> paid 4 sous per day.[42]

---

[42] Voltaire, *Epîtres, stances et odes*, Epître XLIII (London, 1779).

When Villars received news of Belle-Isle's death, he exclaimed, "That man has always been luckier than me!"[43] He was not to wait long. He himself died a natural death, on 17 June. Philipsburg fell on 18 July. A celebratory *Te Deum* was composed by Colin de Blamont. It was performed at the Chapel of Versailles during the Royal Mass.

On 14 December, Colonel de Lenck, who owned the regiment, died at the Château de Meisenheim as a result of war injuries. Proprietorship was taken over by Pierre Appelgrehn, a Stockholm native who had joined the regiment in 1696. He would be made a brigadier on 1 March 1738. In 1737, the RSR was stationed at Strasbourg. On 18 November of that year, the Treaty of Vienna ended the War of the Polish Succession. Still based in Alsace, the RSR now had only 50 officers and 640 enlisted men. On 8 January 1738, it was reduced to only a single battalion.

Meanwhile, since 1735 Austria had fought a separate war with the Ottoman Empire. In 1739, France offered to mediate between the two historic enemies. On 17 September, the RSR took deployed to Hungary, where it attended the peace settlement between the warring empires. Cardinal de Rohan wrote "Your regiment, Gentlemen, is one of the most eminent in the Kingdom! Valorous conduct in times of war, devotion and fidelity in service, perfect discipline: these are the qualities which form the basis of the appreciation and respect, which we the highest chiefs, have for this superb corps, composed for the most part of members of a nation which has received valor as a heritage, and which has always been a friend of France."[44]

With the reputation of the RSR at its zenith, Count Frederik Axel von Fersen, (father of the Count Axel von Fersen who was later linked to Marie Antoinette), now joined the regiment. He enjoyed a brilliant career with it while still playing a major role in the politics of his native Sweden.

On 1 July 1739, King Frederik I of Sweden sought Louis XV's agreement to reward the regiment with the formal appellation "Royal Swedish Regiment." Formal entreaties came from Count de Tessin and Baron de Flemming, the latter Swedish Minister in Paris. The new designation, conferred officially on 30 October 1742, gave the RSR certain privileges,

---

[43] Th. H. Barrau, *Livre de morale pratique* (Paris, Hachette, 1852), p. 264.
[44] *Mémoires du duc de Luynes sur la cour de louis XV*, Vol. 3 (Paris: 1860), p. 257.

better supplies, and permanent royal favor in both countries. The number of aristocratic Swedish officers active in the RSR increased considerably.

The War of the Austrian Succession

With the death of the Habsburg Emperor Charles V in October 1740, a new *casus belli* soon appeared. France refused to accept his Pragmatic Sanction which had transferred the imperial throne, since he had no sons, to his daughter Maria Theresa, then 23 years old. Following a succession reputedly made up only of parchments and treaties, the warrior king Frederick II of Prussia, who later came to be known as Frederick the Great, famously exclaimed at that time, "It would have been better to have an army of 20,000 men."[45] The military confrontation that ensued became the next major European conflagration, the War of the Austrian Succession (1740-48). Once again, France and its allies were pitted against the Austrian Habsburgs and theirs. A new dimension arose with a militant Prussia on the rise. France did not have as many troops as its adversaries, Prussia came to its aid, supported by French subsidies. Since France, too, was a long-stranding enemy of Russia, this alliance was of great importance not only in Central Europe but in the east as well.

The Royal Swedish Regiment was integrated once again into the army of General Charles-Louis Augusta Fouquet, Count de Belle-Isle, in which Victor François, Duke de Broglie, also played a commanding role. Belle-Isle, as the grandson of the great Fouquet, was a man who had earned the confidence of Cardinal de Fleury and would, following his grandfather, be elevated to the rank of marshal in 1741. Admired at court for his military skills and many valued personal qualities, not least of which was humility, a rare commodity indeed at Versailles, he famously commented, "I have made mistakes, but I have never had the ridiculous pride not to admit it."[46]

When the French guards under Count d'Anterroches encountered the British Royal Grenadiers under Lord Charles Hay at the Battle of Fontenoy, on 11 May 1745, there was a courtly verbal exchange. The French commander exclaimed to the enemy: "Gentlemen of England,

---

[45] Jean-Paul Bled, *Frédéric le Grand* (Paris, Fayard), p. 189.
[46] François-Antoine Chevrier, *La vie politique et militaire du maréchal duc de Belle-Isle* (Van Buren, 1762), p. 195.

would you commence firing."⁴⁷ These noble sentiments belied the horrors that ensued. After the British initiated action, the French troops suffered 98 dead and 313 wounded. The Swiss Guards assisting the French, as well as the Courten Regiment, each lost 200 men. When the battle ended, the French had suffered some 7,000 casualties, against the enemy, whose total was some 10,000.⁴⁸ As Jean-Pierre Bois has put it, in reality, "The war in lace does not exist. The only reality is fear, after which comes courage."⁴⁹ Clearly, then, while these wars were far more limited in scope than later ones, they could be just as intense and deadly in relative terms. As the Marquis d'Argenson put it, "the ground of Fontenoy was covered in human blood and the shreds of human flesh."⁵⁰

On 15 May 1741, the RSR was increased in size by two battalions. Together with Belle-Isle's other forces, it advanced into Bohemia, which was in a state of revolt against the Habsburgs, to join up with Prussian forces. Nonetheless, against this tumultuous backdrop, Maria Theresa was crowned Queen of Hungary, if not yet Holy Roman Empress. On 26 November, French, Saxon, and Bavarian troops occupied Prague. Then, on 24 January 1742, Charles Albert, Elector of Bavaria, was elected Holy Roman Emperor as Charles VII. Maurice of Saxony, under the command of General de Broglie, took Egra. In April and May, an invasion of Bohemia ensued. The Castle of Wodnian was taken, followed by the Battle of Sahay, in which the RSR participated. Charles Gustaf, Baron von Falkenhayn, entered the RSR as an ensign that same year, eventually rising through the ranks to the rank of major in 1747.

With the defeat of the Austrians in Bohemia, Fredrick the Great withdrew his troops from the conflict on 11 June, leaving the French unsupported in Prague. The Austrians took advantage of this situation by laying siege to Prague the following day, with 28,000 men commanded by Field Marshal Prince Johann von Lobkowitz. The French attempt to break out of Prague but failed. It took until 14 September for assistance to arrive under Marshal de Maillebois, finally enabling some of the French to

---

⁴⁷ Voltaire, *Précis du siècle de Louis XV*, in *Œuvres complètes de Voltaire* (Paris, 1883), p. 235.
⁴⁸ Jean-Pierre Bois, *Fontenoy 1745* (Economica, 2012), p. 78.
⁴⁹ Ibid., 29.
⁵⁰ Philipp Portelance, *L'expérience de la guerre au siècle des Lumières (1715-1789)*, p. 24

depart, including the RSR. Colonel Appelgrehn, who commanded the right column, fell in the siege. De Broglie was also in difficulty, under attack by Austrian Hussars, and marched "10 leagues across the plain, having to drag my steps along with 11,000 infantrymen (in quite a state) and 3,250 dilapidated horses."[51] Lobkowitz, in contrast, had 3,000 fine horses and 12,000 infantrymen in good order. The weather was dreadful, and Lobkowitz failed to catch up with the French, who managed to reach Egra.

It was on 30 October 1742 that Louis XV granted his Swedish forces the title of Royal Swedish Regiment, for which it received the same privileges as all royal regiments including the protection of the king, new flags and ordinance, and other privileges. Joseph Magnus de Tossetta, Count de Sparre (1704-87) now became lieutenant-colonel of the regiment, having served in it since 1716. It was the decision of Fredrik I of Sweden to place a Swede at the regiment's head, as I. F. Henry Devon explained in 1786:

> The Royal Swedish Regiment in the service of France gives the opportunity for several young men to go abroad for some time. Those who are destined for the military and, in particular, the navy, are obliged to do service in some powerful foreign state if they want to obtain advancement back home. By this maxim, those who have ambition, and they generally all have it, acquire the desire to learn and to be useful one day to their Fatherland.[52]

Drevon refers to an officer who, in 1778, amalgamated his French responsibilities with those he had in Sweden, writing:

> On 9th September, the King [Gustaf III] announced the dissolution of the Diet (that is, in Sweden) and a new assembly for the year 1778. His Majesty had all the courts notified of the success of this revolution. Baron Lieven, lieutenant in the Swedish Guards and at the same time an officer in the Royal Swedish Regiment of France, was charged with

---

[51] *Correspondance inédite de Victor-François, duc de Broglie, maréchal de France, avec le prince Xavier de Saxe, comte de Lusace, lieutenant-général, pour servir à l'histoire de la guerre de Sept-Ans, publiée par le duc de Brogue et Jules Vernier, archiviste du département de l'Aube*, Vol. 1 (Paris: Albin Michel, 1903).
[52] I. F. Henry Drevon, *Voyage en Suède, contenant un état détaillé de sa population, de son agriculture, de son commerce et de ses finances, suivi de l'histoire abrégée de ce royaume et de ses différentes formes de gouvernement, depuis Gustave I en 1553, jusqu'en 1786 inclusivement, sous le règne de Gustave III* (Université de Gand, 1789), p. 269.

bringing the news to Versailles, for which His Most Christian Majesty granted him the rank of colonel.[53]

On 16 December 1742, Belle-Isle left Prague with some 14,000 men, over a period of ten days, as de Broglie had done, and under appalling wintry weather conditions. François de Chevert stayed in the Bohemian capital with his 6,000 men. He wrote to his Austrian enemy, without mincing words, "I wish to inform your general that if we are not accorded the honors of war, I will set fire to the four corners of Prague and my sepulcher will be its ruins."[54] Chevert received a positive reply and was authorized to withdraw, thereby capitulating Prague to the Austrians.

In early 1743, two battalions of the RSR joined the troops of Marshal de Coigny.[55] On 18 January, the RSR took part in the defense of Egra. On 27 June, however, Marshal Noailles was defeated by the British, Hanoverians, and Austrians at the Battle of Dettingen, in Bavaria, in the last battle in which a British monarch – George II – led his troops. In celebration of this Allied victory, George Frederick Handel composed and performed his famous Dettingen *Te Deum*. Nevertheless, Egra fell to the Austrians and the French, and were compelled, with the RSR, to retreat toward Alsace and France. Lieutenant Poiret, a grenadier serving with the RSR, was able to save the treasury of Broglie's army, worth some 100,000 golden Louis.

On 15 March 1744, France declared war on Britain. Soon after, on 5 April, Prussia gave friendly signals to France, distressed at Austrian successes in Silesia, a province Frederick II meant to annex. Thus emboldened, on 16 April, France also declared war on Austria. That July, the RSR returned to Alsace under the command of Marshal de Coigny. Together with other French troops, they retook Wissembourg. Nearby, they saw action along the fortifications along the River Lauter. This culminated in battles at Augenheim and Donauwörth.

By 1 September, the RSR was back in Bavaria. It then retreated towards the Rhine, taking Freiburg im Breisgau after a two-month siege.

---

[53] Ibid., p. 420.
[54] Enrico Cornet, *Siège de Prague (1742)*, Tendler, 1867), p. 68.
[55] Duc de Noailles, *Campagne de Monsieur le Maréchal Duc de Noailles en Allemagne, l'an MDCCXLIII0* (1743), p. 330.

In celebration of this and other victories, a *Te Deum* by Colin de Blamont, Superintendent of the King's Music, was composed in October. The Duke de Luynes called it "an excellent piece of music, bearing the mark of the great masters."[56] In Paris, the king commanded Charles-Gaspard Guillaume de Vintimille du Luc, Archbishop of Paris, to have the *Te Deum* sung to express his gratitude to God for "having more than seconded my efforts and enabling me to triumph at the head of my armies."[57] The archbishop in turn ordered his clergy to organize celebrations in order to "thank the God of the Armies for the various favors he has showered upon the King and particularly for the significant conquest which this Prince, barely returned from the gates of death, has carried out with such courage."[58] In the Chapel Royal of Versailles, a *Te Deum* was sung, composed by Henri Madin, Assistant Master of the King's Music.

By early December 1744, the RSR found itself in action in the Battle of Schellenberg, by Donauwörth, where another great battle had been fought between France and its enemies forty years before. The Swedish nobleman Olof von Stierneman (1725-1808) now became company chief and was made a knight of the Order of the Sword and the French Royal Order. He would later return to Sweden where he became a noted author in the French language.

On 15 April 1745, the RSR was transferred to the command of General de Ségur and participated in the defeat which took place at the Battle of Pfaffenhoffen, in Bavaria, against the Austrians. Ségur then retreated towards Bavaria.

On 1 May, Joseph Magnus de Tossetta, Count de Sparre, who had been commanding colonel of the RSR was given a brigadier's certificate. Ten days later, Maurice of Saxony, allied to France, defeated the British, Dutch, and Austrians. On 31 May, the RSR rejoined the French Army of the Lower Rhine. Another Swedish aristocrat, Per Scheffer, younger brother of Ulrich Scheffer, obtained a captain's certificate in the regiment.

---

[56] Charles-Philippe d'Albert, duc de Luynes, *Mémoires du duc de Luynes sur la cour de Louis XV (1735-1758)* (Paris, 1865), p. 148.
[57] "Mandement de monseigneur l'archevêque de paris, qui ordonne que le Te Deum sera chanté dans toutes les églises de son diocèse...prise de la ville de Fribourg" (Paris, 1744).
[58] Ibid.

The RSR then reattached itself to the army commanded by the Prince de Conti, a member of the princely house Bourbon-Condé, in the Netherlands. The following July, it participated in the sieges of Mons and Charleroi. Thereafter, from 6-30 September, it was present at the victorious siege of Namur, where it had rejoined the army of Maurice of Saxony. On 11 October, Maurice one again defeated the British, Dutch, and Austrians, at the Battle of Rocourt, in today's Belgium, with the help of the RSR. A captain Ettelingen of the regiment lost his leg in action. Maurice had exhorted his troops, "Whether or not the attacks are successful, the troops must remain in whatever position they find themselves at night in order to assail the enemy once again."[59]

In particular, the RSR distinguished itself during an attack by the village of Ans, where, as Maurice put it, "the infantry has conducted themselves with such valor that it deserves the highest praise."[60] On 12 November, the RSR was enlarged by four battalions. Lieutenant Ulric Scheffer now received permission to return to Sweden to participate in a convocation of the Swedish diet. When he returned, he was informed that his brother's solicitation had achieved his elevation to the rank of colonel.

In early 1747, the RSR was stationed first at Namur and then at Huy. In April, Captain Lilliehöök, a Swedish officer in the French service, obtained from d'Argenson a certificate making him lieutenant-colonel of the RSR. As d'Argenson noted at the time, "His Majesty is determined to do so all the more willingly as he is ready to give on all occasions marks of the consideration He has for the Prince Royal of Sweden (Adolf Fredrik), of whose protection you are grateful. You have testified that this officer is particularly honored."[61]

On 1 July 1747, it was decided to increase the number of Swedish gentlemen active in the RSR. To this end"

> His Majesty, having resolved to make further increases in his troops, has issued 5 ordinances to increase by one battalion each of the regiments, etc. ... That H. M. having by his Ordinance of November 12, 1746, made various increases in the Royal-Swedish regiment, in order to place the

---

[59] Maurice de Saxe, *Les Rêveries, La Haye* (1756), p. 167.
[60] Ibid.
[61] RA, *Diplomatica Gallica,* Vol. 340, "Lettre de d'Argenson à C. F. Scheffer, 27 avril 1747," from C. Wolff, *Vänskap och makt*, pp. 175-181.

gentlemen of this nation who wished of employment in its troops, and wishing to further promote several of those who are currently maintained only as second officers, or officers reformed after this regiment, he has deemed it appropriate to increase the German infantry regiment of Fersen by one battalion composed of 660 men.[62]

On 2 July, the RSR participated in the Battle of Lauffeld. Then, in August, Fredrik von Fersen received the king's agreement to advance the Swedish Count de la Garde, a brother-in-law of Count Ekeblad, and Baron Torwigge, nephew of Wrede. Fersen wrote:

> It is assumed that the King's intention in granting such favor to the Swedish nation is to build up a strong party in the Swedish nobility which through the country's constitutions influences political affairs. If this is the case, it seems that not enough attention can be paid to the choice of those to whom they are distributed. Count Delagardie and Baron de Torvigge, one brother-in-law of Count Ekeblad, senator of Sweden, and the other nephew of Senator de Wreden, are among those who deserve to have preference over their compatriots ... as much in relation to their birth and personal merit as in relation to their kinship, who, exercising the first dignities in Sweden, is able every day to be useful to the king in the senate of Sweden.[63]

By 1748, the RSR numbered some 2,846 men, maintained at a cost of 772,104 livres per year.

Count Fredrik von Fersen, the old superior officer of Ulrich Scheffer, Marshal of the Noble Estate of the Swedish Diet, obtained gratifications (advancement and money) for his friend, "in consideration of the services which he has provided as a Swedish employee, in the service of His Majesty."[64] It was Fersen, who, in his role as colonel of the RSR, proposed the advancement of his regiment to the Minister of War. He noted at this time the birth, origin, and religion of his officers, their family relationships, and their political interests.

In April and May, 1748, the RSR took part in the siege of Maastricht. On 11 April, a large French army, stationed at Tongres, in the Meuse

---

[62] Jacques Bernard, *Lettres historiques: contenant ce qui se passe de plus important en Europe et les réflexions nécessaires sur ce sujet.* Vol. 123 (Ghent, 1747), p. 323.
[63] RA, Stafsundsarkivet, "Axel von Fersen," d.ä.:s arkiv. Vol. 14, "Lettre d'Axel von Fersen à d'Argenson," 2 février 1748.
[64] Ibid.

valley, was heading towards Maastricht under the command of Maurice of Saxony. By 15 April, the army encircled the town. Over the next week, they heavily bombarded it. On 29 April, Maurice gave the order for a general assault. According to the laws of war, a town that does not surrender and is taken by assault suffers the looting and massacre of the garrison, but Lord Sackville, aide-de-camp to the Duke of Cumberland, postponed the surrender of the town and the assault did not take place. Finally, the city surrendered on 7 May. Three days later, Joseph de Sparre was promoted to Field Marshal.

With hostilities at an end, the regiment was reduced to three battalions on 26 December and, on 1 February 1749, to two.

In November 1750, the RSR wen into winter quarters at Göttingen. Maurice of Saxony died on 30 November. On 7 February 1751, his body was transferred to Strasbourg Cathedral, where it was ceremonially received and granted an honor guard:

> The garrison shortly before had taken up arms, part of it had been placed in the streets, through which the convoy was to pass, to go alongside the guard of honor. The surplus troops had remained with their flags around the cathedral. At three o'clock, they took on the role of colonel and directed their march through the Rue des Orfèvres towards the new church, saluted by parading in front of the tomb, and continued their march, the cavalry at the head, over the 'tailors' bridge' and the Rue de la Mésange, walked along the Pfennings Tower, along the arcades and went through the Rue des Serruriers in St. Thomas, whence with redoubled steps they crossed the bridge of St. Thomas, lining up on the quays of St. Louis, namely the dragoons of Jarnac on foot, Salis and the Royal Swedish Regiment on the quay to the right of the bridge; Beauce, the Royal Corps, Alsace and Lionnais on the one on the left, the Colonel General's cavalry regiment returned to its quarters.[65]

By 10 October, the RSR was stationed in Phalsbourg, in the north-east of France:

> According to the latest announcements from Alsace, the troops which must compose the garrisons of this province during the winter, include 37 battalions, 7 regiments of cavalry and 2 of dragoons: They will be distributed as follows, in accordance with the orders received from the

---

[65] "Relation de la Pompe funèbre à l'occasion de la translocation du corps de M. le maréchal de Saxe dans l'église St. Thomas" (Bibliothèque de l'Etat de Bavière, 1777), p. 6.

War Office, namely...in Phalsbourg the Royal-Swedish and Frisian regiments, cavalry.[66]

In early 1752, Captain Per Scheffer was granted a royal patent promoting him to colonel, while in May Count de Sparre was named a Commander of the Royal and Military Order of St. Louis.[67] On 6 September 1754, Alexander de Sparre, the eldest son of Joseph de Sparre, was named the proprietor colonel of the RSR, with the consent of Louis XV, to take effect in 1756, after his father resigned his command.

In 1755, Joseph de Sparre, in his treatises of military instruction, gave his opinion with respect to the debate which put partisans of columns in opposition to those who preferred thin lines. He advocated a mixed order: "M. Folard makes sufficiently clear the advantage of an attack by column; but this advantage seems to me still greater, when the columns are supported by a line in battle."[68]

---

[66] J. T. du Breuil, "Amsterdam: avec privilège de nos seigneurs, les états de Hollande et de West-Frise," 1751.
[67] *Suite de la Clef, ou Journal historique sur les matières du temps*, Volume 354, (1752).
[68] Jean-Lambert-Alphonse Colin, *L'infanterie du XVIIIe siècle: la tactique* (1907), p. 284.

Chapter 4:

The first global wars

The Seven Years War 1756-63

After Maria-Theresa's accession to the Habsburg throne, the question of Silesia remained open. Prussia, under Frederick the Great, had conquered Silesia during the War of the Austrian Succession, and the Austrian monarch had never accepted this. France supported Prussia and, moreover, was in every greater confrontation with Britain since 1713, because of their competing American colonies. Britain was, of course, still an ally of Austria, and looked with trepidation on France's vast Louisiana Territory, which spanned North America and effectively blocked further British expansion westward. France's domination of the fur trade, exploitation of fishing areas near British territory, and frontier politics also created ever growing friction. As a result, this confrontation soon erupted into war, arguably the world's first global conflict, stretching from India in the east to Canada in the west.

The RSR was now incorporated into the French army as the 95th Regiment and was stationed at Dunkirk. Per Scheffer, its colonel, obtained a pension of 1,200 livres, to be paid out of the royal treasury, for "the attachment which the gentlemen his brothers have shown on all occasions for his person, and for the interests which unite France and Sweden."[69]

France declared war on 23 January 1756. On 22 January, Joseph de Sparre relinquished his proprietorial rights over the RSR in favor of his eldest son, Alexander Toffeta, Count de Sparre de Kronemberg.

In 1757, French troops, including the RSR which rejoined the army of the Lower Rhine, prepared for an invasion of Hanover, under the

---

[69] *Diplomatica Gallica*, Vol. 355, "Lettre de d'Argenson au chargé d'affaires Sven Bunge," 6 juin 1756.

command of Louis-Charles César le Tellier, Duke d'Estrée, who was about to become a Marshal of France. He was a grandson of Louvois and had served under the Marshals Berwick and Maurice de Saxe, and was known for his skills in maneuvers, albeit often with little progress. By 16 April, it was in Cologne and in June, at Bielefeld, with the principal corps.

On 26 July, a French victory was achieved at Hastenbeck, near Hanover, in which the RSR formed the principal columns on the left flank. Lieutenant Dahlstierna was killed and Captain d'Alheim was wounded. General François de Chevert, who led the men in battle, announced victory to his commander, who was on the verge of ordering a retreat. Later that month, a celebratory *Te Deum* was sung at the Royal Chapel at Versailles, composed by Colin de Blamont. This victory opened the way to the conquest of Hanover and Minden. In its wake, d'Estrée was replaced by Marshal de Richelieu, who had earned the nickname *"le mayonnaise."* This was a dish, now the famous condiment, which had been created for him to celebrate another battle, that of Mahón.

On 5 December, Frederick the Great of Prussia triumphed over the Austrians at the Battle of Leuthen. His army had been deployed using an oblique order of battle, in contrast to the thin lines of the enemy, and was reinforced by a ring movement, in the wings of which one exerted the greatest pressure, thereby achieving an amazing advantage. By doing so, the enemy line was easily broken and brought under fire from behind. Shortly thereafter, as the new year approached, the RSR took up its winter quarters at Neustadt-am-Rübenberge, where the second lines had been.

By early 1758, the war was bogged down. At the end of January, Louis XV sent his army, including the RSR and under the Count de Clermont, again to Bohemia, to harass the Austrians. Clermont was a member of the cadet branch of the Condé family, a prince of the blood, and also a brother of the Duke de Bourbon. The commendatory abbot of Saint-Germain-des-Prés, he was known as the "General of the Benedictines" and was also a great friend of Madame de Pompadour, the King's official mistress. His connections were of the highest order, but, alas for his troops, his military prowess and gifts were negligible. Nevertheless, he succeeded in reestablishing order and discipline, which had become increasingly lax under his predecessors. A popular ditty of the time expressed it so:

Half plume, half jabot,
As unfit for one as for the other,
Clermont fights like an apostle
And serve his God as well as he fights.[70]

By February 1758, the Allied Army, under the command of Ferdinand of Brunswick, commenced a winter offensive in the German lands. The RSR retired to the Rhine with the rest of the French forces. From 30 March to 4 April, it reformed by Wesel, on the second line of the army of Clérmont. Eventually, on 12 June, it took part in the Battle of Allen, near the Rheinfeld Canal.

On 3 June, Clermont's forces, including the RSR, were surprised by an attack carried out by Ferdinand of Brunswick and his army. At the resulting Battle of Krefeld, Clermont's forces occupied a commanding position. He did not make use of it, however. As an observer sarcastically noted, "It is certain that Monsieur de Clermont was at table at one o'clock, that he had lost the battle before six o'clock, that he arrived in Reims at 10:30 and went to bed at midnight; he has done well in a short period of time."[71] His baggage train was captured, including his menagerie of pet monkeys, "learned dogs," budgerigars and trained crows, not to mention a tribe of chefs and female dancers. Clermont's foibles notwithstanding, the RSR covered the retreat with brio. At the end of July, it was transferred first to the army of Marshal Louis-Georges-Érasme de Contades, and then to that of Marshal Charles de Rohan-Soubise, where it reassembled with other troops near Friedberg, in Hesse-Kassel.

On 23 July, the RSR contributed to the victory of the Duke de Broglie at Sandershausen, in Hesse, after which nearby Kassel was conquered. Later, on 10 October, the regiment took part in the victorious Battle of Lutterberg, against the armies of Hesse-Kassel and Hanover. Soubise, who had commanded but not actually taken part in the military engagements there, was nonetheless made a Marshal of France by Louis XV, leading to the quip:

---

[70] Barthélemy-François-Joseph Mouffle d'Angerville, *Vie privée de Louis XV*, Lyton, 1785, Lyon.
[71] Jean-Pierre Thomas, ed., *Louis de Bourbon Condé, comte de Clermont* (Champs-Elysées Dauville, 2019).

> Why give the baton to Soubise
> when Chevert is the conqueror?
> It is given to the blind man
> And not to the conductor![72]

On 12 April 1759, the RSR joined Broglie's army and took up bivouac near Bergen. The next day, it took part in a major battle there. The RSR was positioned on the first line, on the right flank, under the command of Prince Camille de Lorraine. At about 10 o'clock, it was engaged in putting out a fire which had been caused by the advance of the Allies on Bergen, but which had been blocked. Alexander de Sparre, in particular, distinguished himself in this action.

In July, the regiment was transferred to the command of Count Claude-Louis de Saint-Germain (1707-78). He had studied with the Jesuits and had originally intended to take holy orders. However, in the end, he had bought military commission as a sub-lieutenant. He then left France, it is said, because of a duel. Later, he joined the army of the Elector Palatine, and then that of the Elector of Bavaria, during the War of the Austrian Succession, in 1740, distinguishing himself with great bravery. Thereafter, he returned to France and fought with merit in the Seven Years War.

Although Saint-Germain showed more ability than the other army commanders, and was admired by his soldiers, he was the victim of jealousy and intrigue. He had denounced the vices of the French military system in a 1758 memoir, thanks to his experience in foreign armies and during the war. He eventually retired in 1760 and was named Field Marshal in the Danish army by order of King Frederick V of Denmark, who now charged him with reorganizing the Danish military.

Upon the king's death in 1766, Saint-Germain returned to France, where he settled on an estate in Alsace. A financial crisis dissolved the funds he had saved during his service in Denmark and made him dependent on the good will of the French government. Saint-Germain was then presented at Court by Turgot and Malesherbes, and was appointed Minister of War by Louis XVI on 25 October 1775. He endeavored to

---

[72] Doigny du Ponceau, *Les quatre âges de l'homme, poème en quatre chants* (Delaforest, 1825).

reduce the number of officers and establish order and regularity in the service, radically changed the rules of drill and maneuver, recalled the disgraced General de Gribeauval to reform the field artillery, and introduced the twelve royal military schools by ordinance in March 1776. However, his attempts to introduce Prussian discipline into the French army met with such opposition that he resigned on 23 September 1777 and was replaced by the Prince de Montbarrey. Saint-Germain then accepted a royal pension of 40,000 livres, but died shortly thereafter, on 15 January 1778. Saint-Germain's ideas and methods, although much maligned at the time, exerted a profound influence thereafter, especially after the Revolution swept away the Old Guard.

On 18 January 1760, the infantry was reorganized. This enabled the regiment to increase its size by three battalions, thanks to the incorporation of the Royal Polish Infantry within it. At this stage, the regiment was placed under the command of Friedrich von Bülow. At the end of that month, it took up winter quarters on the first line, near Koblenz. Then, from late March, it was transferred to Koblenz, again on the first line. Specifically, on 23 March, it joined the first line, on the right flank, of de Broglie's brigade. It eventually took part in the Battle of Corbach, on 10 July, under the command of Saint-Germain, who played a heroic role in a counterattack. Alexander de Sparre also distinguished himself. Second Lieutenant Mannerheim, a relation of the future great twentieth-century Finnish Marshal and president, was killed. Captains Ulfsparre and Elgenstierna, as well as eight other officers, were wounded, among them Lieutenants d'Armfeldt, Tideman and Aminoff. Of the enlisted men, 38 were killed and 58 wounded. Thereafter, from 14 July, the regiment took up a position between Bernadotte and the main army.

During November and December 1760, the RSR was stationed near Eisenach. During its stay, an act of espionage was uncovered within the regiment, which led to an exchange between Prince Xavier of Saxony and Marshal de Broglie. The former wrote from Eisenach, on 4 December 1760, "I have the honor to inform you, Marshal, of the arrival of the troops in Eisenach and of their present location. ... Monsieur de Stainville left here, on his departure, a Swedish officer under arrest, who he told me was suspected of being a spy. There is no evidence against him other than that he changed his name and clothes on the road several times. Here is a letter he wrote to M. d'Ulfsparre, captain of Royal-Swedish."[73]

Marshal de Broglie then wrote to Prince Xavier, from Cassel, on 8 December 1760: "I have the honor to address to Monsieur the Count de Lusace the letter I have just received from Sr. de Gronhagen, Major of the Royal Swedish Regiment, by which he will be able to judge that Sr Piper, officer in the service of Sweden, is no longer a suspect and can be released to continue his journey on the passport which the Count of Lusace will kindly send him."[74]

From 30 December, the regiment took up winter quarters at Friedberg.

On 20 July 1761, the RSR was transferred to the command of Michel de Maës. It saw no action that year. In 1762, Louis-Ernest de Sparre, another brother of Joseph, was named colonel commandant of the regiment. On 21 December, after further inaction, it was reduced by royal order, with the other "German" regiments, to only two battalions. Specifically, the king ordered that, "the Regiment of Alsace will comprise three battalions; those of Anhalt, the Mark, Royal Bavarian, Royal Swedish, Nassau and Royal Two Bridges, shall have two battalions."[75]

The Treaty of Paris

On 10 February 1762, the Treaty of Paris finally concluded the Seven Years War. Peace now reigned between France and Great Britain. The latter, however, was now the primary world power and France was the worse off. That said, a principal financial burden from war was now laid on Britain's American colonies, a situation which would undermine their relationship to the mother country and ultimately lead to the American War of Independence.

During the long peace which followed, various officers of the RSR devoted themselves to writing their memoirs. The remaining battalions were transferred in May 1763 to Fort Louis, where they remained until November the following year. They, along with other officers in the service of France became known as the "military luminaries." Their

---

[73] Victor-François de Broglie, op. cit. p. 107.
[74] Ibid., 107.
[75] *Recueil de nouvelles ordonnances militaires, 1767.*

insights and perceptions were to exert a considerable influence on French Enlightenment thinkers of the later eighteenth century and long beyond.[76]

Throughout 1764, the debate over the most efficacious military tactics continued, also within the RSR. Colonel Göran Magnus Sprengtporten's tactical writings of 1752 played a central role. Later, Captain Stierneman, who had participated in some nine campaigns, wrote *Principles of the Art of War*, which pleaded for a return to the ancient model, with less detachment than Folard had suggested: "the different elements of the art of war (excepting those with relation to the navy and engineering) were much better organized by the ancient Romans than they are in our days amongst any of the European powers." Thus, the only way forward was to return to these "principles of the art of war which have not changed since the discovery of gunpowder."[77]

In 1766, Alexander de Sparre was promoted to Field Marshal. In September of that year, Count Curt von Stedingk (1746-1837), a noted military man and significant courtier in Sweden, became lieutenant in the RSR. The following year, 1767, Pierre de Chambge d'Elbhecq was made its commander, a post he only retained until 23 June.

In 1769 the RSR participated in exercises at Verberie, near Compiègne, where the king and his court watched his troops on maneuver, under the command of the Count de Puységur, Field Marshal of the Royal Armies. Thereafter, the RSR retired to the garrisons in Alsace.[78]

On 17 June 1770, the proprietorship of the RSR was purchased by Ludwig Ernst Joseph Sparre, Count de Kronenberg, who also became its commander. However, on 16 April 1771, Carl Gideon Sinclair was appointed commander. Count Curt von Stedingk now became captain in the regiment. The following year, 1772, the important military textbook, *General Essay of Tactics* was published by Guibert. That May, Stedingk became a major in the regiment. In March 1773, he was promoted to the rank of captain-major.

The most significant event at this time was the introduction to the

---

[76] Arnaud Guinier, *L'honneur du soldat, éthique martiale et discipline guerrière dans la France des Lumières*.
[77] Karl Gottlieb Guichard, *Mémoires militaires sur les Grecs et les Romains...commentée par le chevalier de Folard* (Lausanne, 1760).
[78] Pierre Nardin, *Gribeauval: Lieutenant général des armées du roi (1715-1789)* p. 383.

French court of Count Hans Axel von Fersen, Fredrik von Fersen's son, where he immediately impressed with his advantageous physique. He resided at this time with Swedish ambassador, Count de Creutz, who maintained a correspondence with King Gustaf III of Sweden and provided von Fersen with money. He had also provided financial resources to Stedingk and Erik Magnus Staël von Holstein, who were also introduced not only at court, but into the close circles of Queen Marie Antoinette and Madame Necker.[79] Creutz wrote to Gustaf III:

> ...of all the Swedes who have been here in my time, it is he who has been the best received in high society. He has been extremely well treated by the royal family. It is not possible to play a wiser and more decent role than he has done. With the most handsome figure and spirit, he will not fail to succeed in a high society which he has already fully won over.[80]

---

[79] Gustav Philip Creutz, op. cit., p. 351; A. Geoffroy, *Gustave III et la cour de France, suivi d'une étude critique sur Marie-Antoinette et Louis XVI apocryphes*, (Paris, Didier et Cie, 1867), pp. 342-414.

[80] Comte de Creutz, *Lettres inédites de Paris 1766-1770* (Paris, Jean Touzot, pp. 1987, p. 195.

1. Anonymous: Greve Johan Cronhielm af Flosta (1707-1782), portrait in the uniform of the French Regiment of Lenck (future Royal Swedish Regiment), ca. 1730.

2. Joseph Auguste Bruillot (1739-1827): Louis Marie Bizouard de Verny (1773-1794), officer of the Royal Swedish Regiment. (Fonds Grouvel, Royal-Swedish box, Château de Chantilly, Archives du musée Condé. From the *Bulletin Historique du royal-Suédois*).

3. Recruitment panels: Grenadiers du Royal-Suédois. (Fonds Grouvel, Royal-Swedish box, Château de Chantilly, Archives du musée Condé. Original in the collection of the Musée d'Orléans).

4. Nicolas de Largilliere: Marshal Erik Sparre, ca. 1714. Nationalmuseum, Stockholm.

5. Soldier of the Royal-Swedish, ca. 1780. Drawing and painting (Fonds Grouvel, Royal-Swedish cardboard, Château de Chantilly, Archives du musée Condé).

6. Anonymous: Carl Fredrik Armfelt (1730-1787), lieutenant-grenadier at the Royal Suédois in France, 1760. (Fonds Grouvel, Royal-Suédois box, Château de Chantilly, Archives du musée Condé Taken from the *Bulletin Historique du royal-Suédois*).

7. Officer, Royal-Suédois, ca. 1770. (Fonds Grouvel, Royal-Swedish box, Château de Chantilly, Archives du musée Condé. Drawing modeled on an original from the Castanié Collection).

8. Grenadier, Royal-Suédois, 1772. (Fonds Grouvel, Royal-Swedish box, Château de Chantilly, Archives du musée Condé. From the work "Grenadiers des Régiments Foreigners," oil on canvas, collection of Professor Hecht, Faculty of Medicine of Nancy).

9. Fusilier of the Royal-Suédois, ca. 1780. Drawing and painting (Fonds Grouvel, Royal-Suédois box, Château de Chantilly, Archives du musée Condé).

10. Foreign Infantry, 1720s. Magazine plates (Osprey elite uniforms and military history booklet).

11. Royal-Swedish German in 1690 (late 18th century). Handcolored engraving).

12. Carl Frederik von Breda (1759-1818): Portrait of Axel de Fersen, ca. 1800.

13. Colonel Flag of Leisler's Regiment between 1690 and 1694 (From *The Uniforms and Flags of the King's Army*, Marseilles, 1899).

14. Regimental Flag of the Regiment between 1690 and 1760 (From *The Uniforms and Flags of the King's Army*, Marseilles, 1899).

15. Colonel flag of the Royal-Swedish regiment, 1760-1790 (From *The Uniforms and Flags of the King's Army*, Marseilles, 1899).

16. Ordnance flag of the Royal-Swedish regiment between 1760 and 1790 (From *The Uniforms and Flags of the King's Army*, Marseilles, 1899).

17. Soldier of the Royal-Swedish regiment, ca. 1750 (Engraving from the *Bulletin Historique du royal-Suédois*, private collection).

18. Siege of Fort Saint-Philippe, Mahon, 1782 (Engraving from the *Bulletin Historique du royal-Suédois*, private collection).

19. Anonymous: Count Joseph de Sparre (Engraving from the *Bulletin Historique du royal-Suédois*, after the Sparre Collection in Lyon. Private collection).

20. Count Louis de Sparre (1737-1817). (Engraving from the *Bulletin Historique du royal-Suédois*, after the Sparre Collection in Lyon. Private collection).

21. Prame going to the embossing (Engraving taken from the *Historical Bulletin of the royal-Swedish,* according to the Historical Archives of the Ministry of War. Private collection).

Chapter 5:

The American Revolution and its Consequences

The American Revolution (1775-83)

In the wake of growing discontent in Britain's North American colonies, in 1775 revolution broke out when the colonists began to stockpile and defend arsenals. With the advent of military conflict, the revolutionaries were composed of some 5,000 men, as were the colonial militias. The British military, by contrast, were composed of some 50,000 men, of whom 30,000 were Hessian mercenaries. At first, action was limited. George Washington, as commander-in-chief of the American forces, preferred a series of small victories which were easier to achieve than one great one, bearing in mind the overwhelming strength of his enemy.

On 4 July 1776, the colonies in revolt declared themselves independent and united into a new confederation of states, which they called the United States of America. In the wake of these declarations, the colonial forces dramatically increased in strength. On 25 December, Washington and his troops defeated Hessian forces at Trenton, New Jersey, which opened the road to Philadelphia, the greatest city in America. Thereafter, numerous volunteers joined the revolutionary forces. A further victory followed, on 3 January, at Princeton. However, on 11 September 1777, just outside Philadelphia at Brandywine, Washington was checked. On 7 October, however, the Americans were victorious over the British at Saratoga, in upstate New York.

After Saratoga, France realized that it could support the American colonists to aid the defeat of its centuries-old enemy. On 6 February 1778, France signed a treaty of friendship with the revolutionaries. Troops, among them the RSR, were then sent to the north of France in anticipation of being sent to North America. On 28 April, they were placed under the command of Count Hugo Hamilton, the scion of a Scottish family that had emigrated to Sweden many years before. He was "highly recommended by his ambassador, whom he sees often, and whom he introduces into the best houses in society."[81]

Meanwhile, in 1776, Stedingk had become a lieutenant-colonel in the RSR. As a result of the efforts of Necker, Director General of the Royal Finances, the military underwent a strengthening, with a new system for garrisoning the troops, which enabled greater continuity for the army whether they were in war or peace. The RSR returned to France and was based at Saint-Roch, near Montpellier. It then was garrisoned at Avesnes, near Calais.

It was at this point that Axel von Fersen entered the fray. In 1779, King Gustaf III asked him to obtain information on the economic possibilities of trade with the American colonies, or even to buy territory in North America. As a result, Benjamin Franklin wrote to Congress that Sweden had been the first European power voluntarily to offer its friendship to the United States of America, without first being asked. Fersen was keen to join the French expeditionary force in America and Gustaf III, knowing how close his relationship was with the French queen, had him named aide-de-camp to the Count de Vaux, who at this point was expected to take command of the French forces there.

The French troops failed to depart due to the strength of the Royal Navy, however, and Fersen returned to Versailles. There he hastened to the Count de Vergennes and the Minister of War, the Prince de Montbarrey, to ameliorate this situation. On 20 January 1780, he was promoted to colonel and attached to the German infantry regiment of which the RSR formed a part. Then, on 2 February, Rochambeau was appointed to lead the French expeditionary force in America. Lafayette, despite having fought in America earlier, lacked the experience himself to fulfill this role, while de Broglie was deemed too "impulsive" and de Vaux too closely linked to Vergennes.

---

[81] Ministère des Affaires Étrangères, *Contrôle des étrangers*, Archives, vol. 10, p. 9.

French financial contributions to the American forces were originally intended to amount to no less than 5,200,000 livres, a vast sum, but ultimately only 2,600,000 livres arrived. Of this half was in cash, the other half in letters of exchange, as provided by one Monsieur Holker, a banker of Philadelphia. So many young officers were keen to join this force that Louis XVI was obliged to limit their number and choose them himself. The Count de Mercy-Argenteau, the Austrian ambassador in Paris, wrote about this selection process:

> Most of the recent military promotion has come under the auspices of the Queen's protection. All the Polignacs (the queen's friends) played a big part in this occasion, less for them than for their friends, but the latter obtained more than they could reasonably have wished for. The king complacently lent himself to whatever the queen wanted; he himself took care of forming lists which were recast several times according to the intrigues of suitors who obtained changes.[82]

In the final analysis, however, it was Rochambeau who made the final choice:

> Thus Count Charles de Lameth, a very handsome, intelligent subject, who has detail; Mr. Mathieu Dumas, second lieutenant in the Médoc-Infanterie regiment, an excellent draughtsman, who has a military eye, speaks and writes English; finally, Count von Fersen, a Swede, a colonel in the French service, speaks good English, and is highly recommended by the Swedish ambassador.[83]

More precisely, Rochambeau had been in contact with Axel's father during the previous conflicts, which the latter confirms in a letter to his father: "When I spoke to M. de Rochambeau, he told me a thousand honest things, and talked to me for a long time about you, my father; he ended by telling me that he would be delighted to have me near him and to be able to show you how much he esteemed you and was sincerely attached to you."[84]

---

[82] Alfred d'Arneth and M. A. Geffroy, *Correspondance secrète entre Marie-Thérèse et le comte de Mercy-Argenteau*, Vol. 1 (Paris: Elibron Classics, 1874).
[83] *Archives du maréchal de Rochambeau*, Service Historique de la Défense (SHD).
[84] Fersen's letter to his father, 2 March 1780, in Rudolf Maurits Klinckowström, *Le comte de Fersen et la cour de France: Extraits des papiers du grand maréchal de Suède, comte Jean-Axel de Fersen* (Paris: Firmin-Didot, 1877).

In mid February, von Fersen was commissioned made ready to depart. He wrote to his father on 2 March:

> You see me in fulfilment of my wishes, my dear father. We are making a great expedition of 12,000 men, but we are assured that it will be increased to 20,000. I have obtained permission to be part of it as aide-de-camp to the general, who is M. de Rochambeau, but I have been strongly advised to keep it secret, as many others have been refused. Everyone wants to be there and we have made a firm resolution to send only the officers attached to the regiments which are marching. I owe this to M. de Vergennes; he took charge of my case. I am in a state of joy which cannot be expressed.[85]

Rochambeau now organized his troops. His corps consisted of twelve battalions totaling 6,000 men who, it was hoped, would see action along the coast of the United States, rather than in the interior. Nonetheless, the land forces included the Regiment de Bourbonnais, Soissonnais, Saintonge, Royal-Deux-Ponts, the Légion de Lauzun, and the Artillery of the 2nd Battalion of the Regiment of Auxonne. They were to serve as auxiliaries under the military command of George Washington. It was he, rather than Rochambeau or Fersen who would make the decisions with respect to how they would be used. Battlefield tactics, however, remained under Rochambeau, in the first order, and then Fersen. On 4 May, the troops arrived and Fersen linked up with the Duke de Lauzun, who promised him the command of his legion. He also formed links with the Marquis de Ségur, who promised him colonel *en second*. After several weeks at sea, on 20 June they encountered their first British forces – a naval squadron of five ships – and a two-hour battle ensued.

Axel Fersen in America

The best source on Fersen in America, the diary of Baron de Klinckowström, a Swedish colonel, was lost apart from short excerpts. Most of the information that follows comes from Fersen's letters to his father.

On 12 July, Admiral de Ternay's squadron entered the harbor of Newport, Rhode Island, with 6,000 men. Accompanying him were some

---

[85] Ibid.

2,650,000 pounds of ammunition, 25,000 balls, 4,000 bombers, 15,000 quintals of flour, 2,250 quintals of bacon, 6,000 condoms, 10,000 pairs of shoes, 3,000 pints of brandy (alcohol), blankets and bracelets for the Indians, bricks to build bread ovens, canvas for gaiters, thread, and needles.

Fersen and some of the French troops arrived with these troops. Washington was close to New York at this time, and the French troops were waiting for their orders to join him. Offshore, at Gardiners Islands, a few English ships were observing them. After Benedict Arnold treasonously betrayed West Point to the British at the beginning of September, Washington finally asked the French for help. His situation was desperate. He wrote to the French Ambassador Luzerne: "I don't need arguments to convince you of the extremities where our affairs are going and of the need to support them ... You know that, if we are alone, we will be powerless to drive out the English, even to stop their march." Yet Fersen and the French troops stayed in Rhode Island. Although their relations with the Americans were good and their discipline strong, Fersen and his fellow aristocratic officers were bored. He wrote back home, "You know the French, my dear father, and those we call the people of the court, and so can judge the despair in which all our young people of this class are, who are obliged to spend their winter quietly in Newport, far from their mistresses and the pleasures of Paris."[86]

For all that, however, Fersen did admire the life and people of America:

> We saw the most beautiful country in the world, well cultivated, charming situations, well-off inhabitants, but without luxury and without pomp; they are satisfied with the necessities which, in other countries, are reserved only for people of a lower class; their clothing is simple, but good, and their morals have not yet been spoiled by the luxury of Europeans. It is a country which will be very happy if it enjoys a long peace, and if the two parties which at present divide it do not make it suffer the fate of Poland, and of so many other republics.[87]

On 14 September, letters finally arrived from the front, in which Fersen

---

[86] Fersen, Lettre à son père, 08 septembre 1780.
[87] Ibid.

focused on Camden's defeat. Fersen noted in particular, that morale was low: "This, my dear father, is the situation in which we find ourselves, it is not a happy one; it is to be hoped that it will change with the arrival of the second division, which we all await with the greatest impatience. The garrison of Newport is becoming very sad."[88] The situation was tense among the French troops. On 8 September, there was a duel over a trivial matter between M. Dillon and the vicomte de Noailles, who was wounded.[89]

At the end of September, Fersen was to accompany Rochambeau for a meeting with Washington himself. They travelled for three days, during which time the British Admiral Rodney arrived in New York, a fact Fersen and his comrades learned during the course of their travels. During their journey, a curious adventure occurred: one night their carriage wheel broke. Fersen went to ask for help and found a man with a fever who refused: "you could fill my hat with money that you wouldn't make me get up at night." Rochambeau joined them to beg him: "Well, General Washington is waiting for me, you are going to make me miss my appointment, you will be responsible to your country." Hearing Washington's name, the man stood up and put the wheel back on.[90]

The meeting took place on 1 October, at Hartford, Connecticut, with Ternay, Rochambeau, Rochambeau's son, engineering chief de Gouvion, and one other aide-de-camp. Lafayette, who served as an interpreter for Washington, who was accompanied by six American aides-de-camp and twenty-two dragoons.[91]

Fersen described General Washington:

> I had time to see this illustrious man of our century, not to say unique. His beautiful and majestic face, but at the same time gentle and honest, corresponds perfectly to his moral qualities; he looks like a hero; he is very cold, speaks little, but is polite and honest. He has an air of sadness spread over his face, which does not suit him, and which makes him more interesting.[92]

---

[88] Fersen, Lettre à son père, 14 septembre 1780.
[89] Gaston Maugras, *Le duc de Lauzun et la cour de Marie-Antoinette* (Paris: Plon, 1895), p. 220.
[90] Ibid., 221.
[91] Fersen, Lettre à son père, 16 octobre 1780.
[92] Ibid.

On October 16, Fersen, still in Newport, took advantage of a frigate's return voyage to France to report on the situation and to send letters to his father and friends, including Count von Creutz and the Duke de Lauzun. He told his father that he might be tasked with making a trip to France to report on the condition of the troops. However, he did not look forward to this, writing, "I'd rather not be in charge of this chore. Something interesting might happen while I am gone, and it would make me despair not to have been there."[93]

Rochambeau wished to ask Versailles for an increase in forces and money. Morale remained low and everyone dreamed of joining the operations in progress:

> We vegetate at the door of the enemies, in the saddest and most dreadful idleness and inactivity, and we are obliged, by our small number, to take up the tiring role of defense; we are of no use to our allies ... Far from being useful to the Americans, we are a burden to them; we are not reinforcing their army, because we are twelve days' march away from them.[94]

Fersen furthermore explained that lack of cash caused shortages of fodder, and everyone had to buy it at his own expense. Besides, the generals could not agree on how to proceed. He also mentioned a proposal from the Duke de Lauzun, his friend, who offered him the position of colonel, commanding his legion in the Americas, and then to have full ownership of it, some 1,000 men, 500 hussars, and the artillery.

Fersen noted that "The Duke de Lauzun writes to the queen, who has a lot of kindness for him; and she also has a bit for me."[95] Fersen offered the Duke money in exchange for his Legion, concluding: "I don't sell men, though I have bought them sometimes; I would pay myself to find a man to whom I can leave my body, whom I love like my children, with as much confidence as I have in you."[96]

On 26 October, 4,000 men embarked from New York for more southerly destinations: two battalions of grenadiers and chasseurs, as well

---

[93] Ibid.
[94] Ibid.
[95] Ibid.
[96] Fersen, Lettre à son père, 13 novembre 1780.

as detachments of other regiments of the army. Fersen reminds us that the war was very difficult for the British, as well as for the Americans: "What a war for the English, who are obliged to bring everything, even their subsistence! ... this power must have great resources to have been able to sustain it for so long."[97]

Life continued to be boring for Fersen and his men, especially since the war now seemed to be turning to the British advantage. "Their position is good," he wrote, "if they know how to take advantage of it, and ours is hopeless, if it does not change."[98] Fersen still remained hopeful, however. Soon another 6,000 men embarked from New York, including grenadiers and chasseurs, of which 3,000 were to land on the shores of Chesapeake Bay. Their goal was to join the 4,000 Americans sent earlier in order to seize North Carolina and Virginia. As Washington took up winter quarters, on 1 December Rochambeau and Fersen visited these southern states. Fersen lamented, "We saw neither a beautiful country, nor good people; they are, in general, lazy and self-interested; how with these two qualities, are we to take advantage of them for the war?"[99]

By 7 December, Fersen was back in Newport, where the bulk of the French troops were in winter quarters. American successes in the south, meanwhile, caused Lord Cornwallis to withdraw toward the coast, while his troops suffered from fatigue and illness. On 9 January 1781, Fersen and most of the French were still in Newport, maintaining a defensive position, while waiting for reinforcements from Europe. He also spoke of eight ships, including one of 110 guns, three of 80 guns, three of 74 and one of 64. "This is the only way to operate and end a war, for it is ruinous," Fersen wrote in frustration.[100] But for the moment, nothing happened.

By January 14, 1781, fighting in the south had shifted to the Americans' advantage. The insurgent troops, however, were also suffering and demanded the pay which was due to them for the previous fourteen months, as well as food and supplies. Fersen deplored that they had not been paid, as well as the fact that the French themselves lacked money

---

[97] Fersen, Lettre à son père, 26 octobre 1780.
[98] Fersen, Lettre à son père, 13 novembre 1780.
[99] Fersen, Lettre à son père, 7 décembre 1780.
[100] Fersen, Lettre à son père, 9 janvier 1781.

with which to assist them. This led to a worsening of relations between Rochambeau and Washington.

On 3 April, Fersen was still stranded in Newport. Both he and his men were shocked that the South was devastated by English troops, despite the first rumors of success. Fersen wrote:

> This country is not in a position to sustain a longer war, as it is ruined and needs more money and more men. If France does not vigorously come to their aid, they will be obliged to make peace. So far, she has not made any great efforts. For ten months we have been a handful of men on this island and we have not been of any use yet.[101]

Fersen ended up admiring the English troops when he heard of Cornwallis's successes, writing, "This war does honor to the English, although their generals behaved badly in America."[102] In the southern fighting, the British troops benefited from professional training and experience of continental wars.

On 17 May, the French forces continued to await in Newport the reinforcements they were convinced had soon to arrive and were increasingly in a state of preparedness. Nonetheless, Fersen had no news for the command of the Lauzun Legion, which he hoped would allow him to participate in the fighting. This made him ever more impatient:

> I'm starting to get bored with being with Mr. de Rochambeau. He does respect me, it is true, and I am very appreciative of it, but he is defiant in a disagreeable and even insulting way. He has more confidence in me than in my classmates, but his confidence in me is insufficient. Moreover, news does not arrive until very late, because there is a lack of money to pay for a spy in New York.[103]

Additionally, he felt that the French army was in a state of dissipation: "Our army is still as undisciplined as the French army usually is. However, the leaders are very strict, and there is not a day when there are not two or three officers under arrest. I've seen indecent scenes where a whole corps would have deserved to be broken."[104]

---

[101] Fersen, Lettre à son père, 3 avril 1781.
[102] Fersen, Lettre à son père, 11 avril 1781.
[103] Fersen, Lettre à son père, 17 mai 1781.
[104] Ibid.

On 25 May, Washington and Rochambeau met again. Washington wanted to attack New York in a Franco-Americans operation. Rochambeau disagreed and preferred to conduct the operation in Virginia, to the south, around Chesapeake Bay. However, they agreed on one point, namely, that whichever option was chosen, the French must join the Americans north of New York.

French forces finally prepared to depart Newport in order to join the insurgent army, evoking jubilation amongst the troops. The actual campaign plans remained a secret, but Virginia was the goal. The complex military situation can be summarized as follows:

> 1. Rochambeau himself was to remain in Newport with a squadron of six ships.
> 2. Admiral de Grasse in Saint-Domingue (today's Haiti), 3,500 kilometers from Newport, would lead a convoy of 140 ships with some 20 warships.
> 3. Washington would block New York with nearly 10,000 men, facing the English garrison of 13,000.
> 4. The English squadrons patrolled between the Antilles and the coasts of New York.
> 5. Cornwallis was still active in Virginia, commanding about one-third of British forces.
> 6. Before Cornwallis, Lafayette, with American troops, stood ready to attack.

First Phase of the French-American Join Military Engagement

Rochambeau continued to think that an attack in the south would be best.

The men would have to travel 217 miles in fifteen days, with a pack of 60 pounds per man, as well as a musket. Each company was entitled to 1,500 pounds of baggage, which made for twelve wagons per regiment. The officers marched at the head of their men, and Rochambeau demanded that the men's uniforms be checked before entering the villages. The weather was very hot. They would therefore walk at night and in the early morning. Jean-François Coste, the chief doctor of the French troops (and future doctor of Napoleon's Army) gave orders with respect to sanitation, specifically to infuse the water with vinegar and to drink it slowly in small sips, after rinsing ones mouth. Shirts and shoes were to be changed several times and feet soaped in cold water, possibly with a dash of alcohol to harden them.

Captain and cartographer Louis-Alexandre Berthier (the future Marshal of France) followed the French forces as they embarked on 12 June. He remembered "bad roads, wagons overturned, artillery will not arrive until midnight. The army marched in four divisions: Rochambeau, the Vioménil brothers, Custine, Lauzun's cavalry covered the flanks. Forage difficulties. In the evening, music and dance, the women are pretty."[105]

On 6 July, 5,000 French and 3,000 Americans arrived in Philipsburg, New York. The French troops were positioned to the left of the Americans. Washington, outside the city, began to test the English defenses in New York. On 28 July, Admiral de Grasse wrote Rochambeau to tell him that he was going to leave Saint-Domingue for the Chesapeake. This letter, however, did not arrive until 15 August, the day after de Grasse arrived at Newport. Fersen, who had stayed in New England, was sent to hasten the departure of the remainder of the French fleet and the embarkation of artillery from Providence. Then on 15 or 16 August, Rochambeau received de Grasse's late arriving letter and showed it to Washington. They discussed the matter heatedly and decided to lure General Clinton into a trap, by making him believe that an attack on New York was to take place, but, in fact, to attack towards the south in the direction of Yorktown, in Virginia.

On 17 August, the joint Franco-American forces departed Philipsburg, according to plan, and detoured north to cross the Hudson River, bypass New York, and then descend toward Philadelphia. The army arrived at Kings Ferry on 21 August and crossed the river over a period of five days.

Second Phase of the Joint French-American Military Engagement

The French journey to Philadelphia covered some 160km. On 3

---

[105] Louis-Alexandre Berthier, op.cit., p. 1.

September, they arrived in the city and paraded through the town. Fersen wrote, "The troops marched through the city and evoked the admiration of all the inhabitants, who had never seen so many people dressed and armed uniformly, nor so well disciplined."[106]

Admiral de Grasse, meanwhile, arrived in the Chesapeake, with 28 vessels and 3,000 men. They joined the 1,800 men of the Marquis de Lafayette at Williamsburg, Virginia's colonial capital and seat of the College of William and Mary, established in 1693. On 5 September, de Grasse's fleet left the bay to engage the British ships at the Battle of the Capes. The British put up a good fight but withdrew, leaving Yorktown at the mercy of the French and American forces. Cornwallis, therefore, found himself and his 8,000 men left stranded in the city with no help from the sea. Washington and Rochambeau understood this and realized that they had to reach Virginia as soon as possible.

On 7 September, the Franco-American army arrived at the Head-of-Elk-River, at the top of Chesapeake Bay. Due to the loss of many boats, however, most of the troops could not be disembarked. Only the grenadiers and the chasseurs, 800 French and 700 Americans, reached shore. The rest traveled to Annapolis, the capital of Maryland and later home of the United States Naval Academy, to embark on frigates. By the next day, all the French ships had arrived in the Chesapeake and were soon ready to depart for Yorktown. The cavalry was now supported by 1,500 horses, 800 oxen, and 220 wagons that had crossed the Potomac River, at a site where today the Pentagon is situated, in order to reach them. Lauzun and his Legion rushed south, while the rest of the army continued its journey.

On 15 September, Washington wrote of Fersen:

> Dear Sir, Upon information of the sailing of the fleet from the Chesapeake Bay, I gave orders for the troops, who were embarked, to be stopped. Since my arrival at this place, I am informed that Count de Grasse has been joined by Count de Barras, and, having captured two English frigates, has returned to his former station at the Capes. On this pleasing information I have sent forward Count Fersen to hurry on the troops with all possible despatch.[107]

---

[106] Fersen, *Journal des operations*, in Klinckowström, p. 60.
[107] Charles W. Upham, *Life of Washington* (Boston, 1840), p. 45.

On 17 September, Washington, Rochambeau, and de Grasse met near Williamsburg on *Ville de Paris*, flagship of the French fleet. It was decided to hasten the siege of Yorktown because the English fleet, although driven off by Grasse on 5 September, could still return. Therefore, on 26 September, the entire revolutionary army came together in Williamsburg, landing its field artillery and gunners. Two days later, the army approached Yorktown, where Cornwallis was positioned on the right bank of the York River, and Gloucester on the left bank, both surrounded by marshes.

Fersen admired the imposing river, noting that "The river is a mile wide, that is to say a third of a league in France."[108] The French then invested the suburbs of the town, but the Americans were slowed down by the marshes and a damaged bridge, which they were obliged to replace.

Third Phase of the French-American Engagement

Opposing the French and American forces were ten British redoubts manned by 7,000 men. Some 8,000 French and 8,000 Americans confronted them on 30 September. Following an order from General Clinton, who promised to come to Cornwallis's rescue from New York, the English evacuated their advanced works – two large redoubts and a battery of two cannon, separated from the city by a large ravine – and took refuge in the city. The French took over these works, abandoned by the British.

On 6 October, at 8 p.m., the encircling trenches were approximately 600 meters from the town. Now the right flank was positioned up to the river and the left up to a large ravine. The main trench was approximately 1400 meters in length and was defended by four palisaded redoubts and five batteries of cannon. The terrain itself was cut by small ravines, which facilitated attack. On the left, another trench was positioned on the left on the river and on the right on a wood. It contained a battery of four mortars, two howitzers, and two pieces of 24, which, it was hoped, would disturb communications by river between York and Gloucester.

In all, there were 41 guns. The British had less powerful artillery and they acted more defensively, but became more assertive during the day,

---

[108] Fersen, *Journal des operations*, op. cit. p. 57.

for, as Fersen wrote, "they threw a lot of bombs and big royals (big grenades) at us."[109] At night, they established flying, or mobile, batteries.

On 10 October, after work to consolidate the trenches around the town, the Franco-American batteries were ordered to fire. According to British deserters, the artillery was highly effective. Fersen wrote, "our bombs were having the greatest effect and that the number of dead and wounded was increasing considerably."[110]

During the bombardment, the new French army cannon, the "Gribeauval" model, was fired for the first time. Napoleon would later favor it. From the night of 11-12 October, an opening in the second trench, at approximately 250 meters, was carried out by the French, but they were obliged to stop because the British manned two forts that prevented them from going further. Then, at 8 p.m. on 14 October, the French attacked the first British redoubt with some 400 men, grenadiers, and chasseurs, supported by 1,000 men taking "sword in hand." Inside, the attackers found 160 men, British and German. The Americans, meanwhile, took the second redoubt.

Later that evening, Cornwallis sortied 2,000 men from York to go over the river to Gloucester, where he sought reinforcements that failed to arrive. Nonetheless, on the night of 15 October, the British continued to shoot. On the morning of 16 October, they attempted another sortie with 600 men. Although they captured a battery, their assault was repelled, even though, according to Fersen, the French were in a state of exhaustion: "Our soldiers, who had been extremely tired since the beginning of the siege, had been asleep and were surprised."

The siege force had been successful, however, and on 17 October, a parliamentarian was sent to meet Corwallis to negotiate the terms of capitulation. On 18 October, the American, French, and British leaders drafted the official act of surrender. The formal ceremony was scheduled for the next day. British forces departed, surrounded by the line of the Franco-American army.

General Charles O'Hara, at the head of the British forces, had replaced Cornwallis who did not wish to humiliate himself. However, he was

---

[109] Ibid., p. 61.
[110] Ibid., p. 61.

present and Washington, Rochambeau, and La Fayette took part. O'Hara dismounted and handed his sword to Rochambeau, but Dumas, his aide-de-camp, pointed him in the direction of Washington, demonstrating that the British preferred to hand over their weapons to the French, rather than to the Americans, the latter being traitors, that is, insurgents, to them.[111] (Years later, in 1792, O'Hara would again be taken prisoner by the French, in that case by Napoleon at the siege of Toulon). An exchange then took place in which the British returned the son of Rochambeau, a prisoner-of-war, in exchange for O'Hara.

To secure the operation's success, the Duke of Lauzun's Legion was on guard in Gloucester. For Fersen, Cornwallis's conduct was largely faultless. However, he was convinced that, "the only fault that Lord Corwallis made was to stay in York, an action for which really General Clinton was responsible. He had ordered him to do so and he had merely obeyed."[112]

Among the British forces taken prisoner, there were some 7,600 men, 2,000 of whom were ill and 400 wounded. Also seized were 400 dragoon horses, 174 guns, and 40 boats, the majority of which were sunk or damaged. Casualties were reckoned at 274 killed or wounded, including ten officers.[113]

After the siege, Duke de Lauzun reported to Ambassador Creutz, "Count von Fersen showed the most brilliant courage everywhere in the trenches as well as during the attacks."[114] On 23 October, Fersen remained in Yorktown, which became his winter quarters, and wrote his account of the siege of the town, the physical aspects of which he held in low esteem: "It is a nasty little town that looks more like a village."[115]

There were fears that the war was not over. Indeed, there were rumors about continuing military operations, including a possible siege of Charleston, South Carolina, on the coast to the south. Therefore, the French began requesting reinforcements. Fersen was determined to carry

---

[111] Raymond Bourgerie and Pierre Lesouef, *Yorktown, 1781* (1992).
[112] Fersen, *Journal des operations*, p. 62.
[113] Ibid. p. 62.
[114] Maugras, *op. cit.* p. 50.
[115] Fersen, Lettre à son père, 23 octobre 1781.

on. "I only fear peace," he wrote, "and I wish for it to not yet come."[116] Fersen also wished not to follow in the footsteps of his fellow officers, who returned to France to reap the fruits of their glory. This was not to his liking, not least because of the financial expense this would involve:

> All our young court colonels are leaving and will spend their winter in Paris. Some will come back; the others will stay, and will be greatly surprised that they are not made brigadiers, for having been at the siege of York; they believe they have done the most beautiful thing in the world. I will stay, I would have no other reason for going to Paris than for fun and pleasure; they must be sacrificed. My business will be done without me; I would spend money on it; I must spare it. I would rather use it to do some more campaigning here, and to finish what I have started.[117]

In mid December, Fersen and his comrades learned the news of the French defeat at the Battle of Ushant. The convoy commanded by Admiral Guichen, which had been tasked with supplying the American front, was captured and dispersed, a terrible loss that Fersen lamented.

On 4 March 1782, Fersen was in Philadelphia. He departed five days later with the Chevalier de la Luzerne, the French ambassador. Returning to Williamsburg, Fersen provided a description of their journey and Virginia itself, by no means favorable:

> We had a delightful journey, and the canteens which he [the Chevalier de Luzern] had brought with him and which were well stocked with patés, hams, wine and bread, prevented us from perceiving the misery which reigned in the inns, where one finds only salt and no bread. In Virginia they only eat cakes made from Turkish wheat flour, which are roasted a little in front of the fire; it hardens the crust a bit, but the inside is just uncooked dough. They only drink rhum, that is, sugar brandy mixed with water; this is called grogg. Apples have been in short supply this year, which has kept them from having cider. Some 250 miles from here, in the part of Virginia called the Mountains, it's a completely different matter. The country is richer, it is there that the great culture of tobacco is grown, and the land produces wheat and all kinds of fruit, but in the part which borders the sea, called the Plain, where we are, only Turkish wheat is grown. The main production of Virginia is tobacco; it is not that this province, which is the largest of the 13, is not susceptible

---

[116] Ibid.
[117] Ibid.

to other cultures, but the laziness of the inhabitants and their vanity are a great obstacle to industry.[118]

Of the character of the people of Virginia Fersen wrote:

> It does indeed seem that Virginians are a different race of people, for instead of looking after their farms and trading, every owner wants to be a lord. Never does a white man work, but, as in the islands, all the work is done by black slaves who are watched over by whites, and there is a steward at the head of it all. There are in Virginia at least 20 blacks for every white man; this is why this province maintains but few soldiers in the army. All those who trade are regarded there as inferior to others; they say that they are not gentlemen and they do not want to live in society with them. They have all the aristocratic principles and, when one sees them, it is difficult to understand how they were able to enter into the general confederation and accept a government founded on a perfect equality of condition. However, the same spirit that led them to free themselves from the English yoke might well lead them to other steps, and I would not be surprised to see Virginia detach herself, in peace, from other states. I wouldn't even be surprised to see the American government become a perfect aristocracy.[119]

Fersen left Williamsburg on 27 May in the company of de Luzerne and Rochambeau, visiting Portsmouth and Cape Henry. By then he had learned of de Grasse's defeat in April at the Battle of the Saintes, off Guadeloupe, in the Caribbean, where de Grasse had proceeded on his way to attack British Jamaica. For them, this was unfortunate news since the land campaign had depended on de Grasse's ships and might need them again. As Fersen put it, "This one [setback] is considerable and renders the whole campaign void. It gives the English superiority in the islands. If they conduct themselves well, they could do us great harm there, and a reinforcement of troops from Europe could well cause us to lose our conquests." In addition, intense heat and humidity was beginning to return as summer approached: "the heat is already excessive; so one can only judge what it will be in July and August."[120]

Fersen had no further news from Lauzun and his Legion. On 16 July, however, he was back in Philadelphia with Rochambeau and Washington,

---

[118] Fersen, Lettre à son père, 25 mars 1782.
[119] Ibid.
[120] Fersen, Lettre à son père, 27 mai 1782.

where they discussed upcoming military operations. As a result, it was decided that Fersen should travel in secret back to Yorktown to embark the siege artillery for operations aimed at recapturing New York. They then had to sail up the Chesapeake to Baltimore, where Rochambeau would be waiting.

On 19 July, Fersen left for Yorktown but due to illness returned to Philadelphia with the Chevalier de Chastellux. They were received by his great friend the Chevalier de Luzerne, who saw that he was treated. A couple of weeks later, on 8 August, the army was at Baltimore, but Fersen was still in Philadelphia. He waited there for the army to arrive and then followed it to the Hudson river. Unfortunately, in the intense heat, the streams were dry and the army was running out of water. It was now that Fersen affirmed that the campaign of 1782 was not a success. There was, moreover, no news from France.

By August 17, there were considerable delays. Fersen was still waiting for the army to arrive in Philadelphia from Baltimore. In any case, he believed the operations would be tough and tiring:

> It looks like we will only have a tough and tiring campaign this year. The off-season marches and camps are awful in this country. There are continual rains, and the roads are almost impassable. They are probably the only enemies we will have to fight this year.[121]

There were now rumors of an imminent peace. Fersen noted that "England seems to be very inclined in that direction, as long as France is modest in its demands." Moreover, King George himself wanted an end to hostilities, for "General Carleton, who commands in New York, has sent to General Washington a very polite letter, in which he writes him that the king, his master, has granted independence to America."[122]

With hostilities concluding, Fersen began to think of his return to Europe: "This idea causes universal joy, it gives me pleasure that I cannot express; the hope of seeing you again, my dear father, gives me a pleasure that can only be felt."[123]

---

[121] Fersen, Lettre à son père, 17 août 1782.
[122] Ibid.
[123] Ibid.

In September, Fersen and the army were again on the march, crossing the Delaware and the Hudson, near New York. Although it was still hot, they were thinking of taking winter quarters. With the evacuation of Charleston, the British no longer had any presence in the colony outside New York. On 3 October, Fersen wrote from the Crompond camp that "the cold is starting to be keenly felt" and noted living conditions that remained difficult: "I have a tent this year, and a straw mattress; I am rather lacking for blankets, but the coat makes up for it."[124]

In mid October, Queen Marie-Antoinette allowed Fersen's promotion to second colonel of the Royal-Deux-Ponts regiment. At the end of the month, Fersen and the army were stationed in Hartford, Connecticut, for eight days, awaiting Admiral de Vaudreuil's fleet in neighboring Rhode Island. On 4 November, they began their journey back to Providence, arriving on 10 November. Fersen briefly went to Newport to say goodbye to his friends and acquaintances and boarded for Boston. On 20 November, Rochambeau left Providence for Philadelphia, from which he embarked for France, a loss felt by the whole of his army. On 30 November, Fersen boarded the *Brace*. The fleet was now commanded by the Chevalier d'Amblimont, who was not known for his bravery in battle. Fersen, who was still young and very brave himself, put it thus: "He behaved very badly on April 12 (naval battle of Saintes). He ran away instead of obeying the signals ... Still, he is kind, very polite and he has a good ship. I myself am well accommodated and the food is very good."[125]

Fersen thought the fleet would rally Don Galvez's Spaniards and again proceed toward Jamaica. Yet he also believed that he would return to France before the summer 1783. In the event, everyone seemed annoyed by the idea of going to the Caribbean because the commander who would replace Rochambeau, Baron de Viomenil, was reputedly "quick-witted and hot-headed, he does not have the precious composure of M. de Rochambeau."[126] Fersen continued that Rochambeau had been an excellent leader during the war, marvelously ensuring that relations

---

[124] Fersen, Lettre à son père, 3 octobre 1782.
[125] Fersen, Lettre à son père, 30 novembre 1782.
[126] Ibid.

between the French and Americans would be a success. Indeed, he felt that:

> He was the only man who was able to command us here, and to maintain that perfect harmony which reigned between the two nations so different in their manners and their language, and which, deep down, do not like each other. There have never been any disputes between our two armies during the time we have been together, but there have often been just grounds for complaint from us.[127]

Fersen also reported on what characterized bad relations with the Americans:

> Our allies have not always behaved well towards us, and the time we have spent with them has taught us not to like or esteem them. M. de Rochambeau himself has not always had praise for them; in spite of this his conduct has always been the same. His example impressed his army and the harsh orders he gave restrained everyone and so they observed this rare discipline which is admired throughout America, and by the English who witnessed it. M. de Rochambeau's wise, prudent and simple conduct has done more to reconcile America to us than four battles won could have done.[128]

Communications were poor and they still awaited news from Charleston to find out if the English had evacuated the city. In any case, the Duke de Lauzun's Legion was to remain in America, in Wilmington, Delaware (near Philadelphia), until peace was established. Fersen appreciated Lauzun greatly: "I cannot tell you, my dear father, how much I am attached to the Duke de Lauzun and how much I love him. He is the most noble and most honest soul I know."[129]

On 22 December, the French fleet departed Boston for the Caribbean. The voyage lasted until 10 February 1783. The sailing, Fersen wrote, was "long, sad, and boring," with storms, fights, and even the loss of some of the ships: "The impossibility of keeping busy on board, always being in the same room with 45 people, was awful. It's a horrible way of life. The navy is a nasty job, especially in France."[130]

---

[127] Ibid.
[128] Ibid.
[129] Ibid.
[130] Fersen, Lettre à son père, 13 février 1783.

On 3 January, French forces received letters from Madrid, predicted peace. On 13 February, Fersen arrived in Porto-Cabello, the Spanish colony southeast of Curaçao, on the northern coast of South America, remaining there for several weeks. He disliked it, and those he found there:

> Porto-Cabello is a nasty place, which presents no resources of any kind ... If Porto-Cabello were in other hands than the Spanish, it could be made into one of the most beautiful settlements on the coast of South America, but the government does not wish to open its eyes to its own advantage. Everywhere, it wants to force trade and impose restraints. However, to make it flourish, it needs the greatest freedom.

Fersen certainly was keen to either return to Europe or to return to war, but inactivity annoyed him immensely. By June, when it was clear the war was over, Fersen had returned to Versailles. There, he gave thanks to Swedish King Gustaf III and French Queen Marie-Antoinette, finally becoming both commander and owner of the Royal Swedish Regiment.

Swedish Officers in the American Revolution

Some 70 Swedish officers took part in the American War of Independence. A document prepared for the bicentennial of George Washington's birth in 1932 discussed them:

> The majority ... saw service in the United States or in North American waters. One of these, Count von Fersen, distinguished himself as an aide to Rochambeau, and took an active and responsible part in the preparations for the siege at Yorktown. This young nobleman, together with his countryman, Col. Curt von Stedingk, later made a count, were elected to the Order of the Cincinnati, of which society George Washington was the first president. Alongside these illustrious names are those of many Swedes who served in lesser capacities but whose contributions entitle them to recognition. Among these are Baron von Fock who distinguished himself at Yorktown; Baron Nordensk Jöld, who participated in the siege at Savannah and later became vice admiral in the Swedish Navy; Magnus Danier Palmqvist, who fought at Pensacola and Yorktown; Carl Raab, killed at Savannah, and many more who can not here be named for lack of space.[131]

---

[131] *Special news releases relating to the life and time of George Washington*, United States George Washington Bicentennial Commission, Vol. 1, 1932.

Among the others we can note the following:

Georg Gustaf Uggla (1742-1825) was a romantic character, a soldier of fortune, at times reckless and irresponsible. At the outbreak of the American revolution he had actually gone to England, whence he traveled to Canada to fight for the British, only to find that Canada was not a center of recruitment. He then went to Suriname, where he embarked aboard an American boat. He enlisted in the American armed forces while en route to Boston. After weeks at sea, his ship was captured by the British. After a difficult captivity, he was freed in a prisoner exchange and came to Philadelphia. He then joined the Polish General Casimir Pulaski's legion and fought in the siege of Savannah. Later, Uggla was attached to the Army of the South and served as adjutant general under Horatio Gates. During the battle of Camden, he was again captured by the British and returned to Sweden some months later.[132]

Count Curt von Stedingk (1745-1837) was another hero at the siege of Savannah. He said, "As brave men, we resolved to conquer or perish." He commanded the left column: "I had the pleasure of planting the American flag on the last trench, but the enemy renewed its attack and our people were annihilated by crossfire." Von Stendingk was wounded in the fighting. On 6 July 1779, he participated in the capture of Grenada and the naval battle against Admiral Byron. He was given the order of the Cincinnati by Washington in 1783.[133]

Adolph Fredrik Pettersèn was elevated to the nobility on account of his American exploits and adopted the name Rosensvärd. He served in the French navy as second-in-command of a ship and later commanded a unit during the siege of Pensacola, Florida. After the battle, "the officers lifted him upon their shoulders and bore him in triumph to [the General]." King Louis XVI of France wrote a personal letter to Gustaf III about Reosensvärd, who was decorated by France as well as Sweden.[134]

Baron Johan Fock (1753-1817) entered the French service in 1778. He became a captain and was later appointed adjutant to the Duke de Lauzun.

---

[132] Amandus Johnson, *Swedish Contributions to American Freedom 1776-1783*, Vol. 2 (Philadelphia, 1957), p. 159-171.
[133] Ibid., 175-176.
[134] Ibid., 181.

He fought at the siege of Yorktown and the Duke of Lauzun said "he showed exceptional bravery and intelligence during a furious cavalry attack, when Duke de Lauzun's hussars defeated a corps of English dragoons twice their number."[135] After the war he migrated to England and then Ireland. Several of his descendants served in the British military all the way up to the World War I.

Captain Christian Sundahl likewise conducted himself brilliantly at Yorktown and was awarded the *Pour le Mérite* for bravery in action.

Johan Magnus Brummer (1754-1824) was an ensign in the Swedish navy and served later in the French navy. In 1781, he embarked on the American frigate *Two Esters*. He helped to capture the English frigate *Frieland* and was wounded in the knee. A few months later, Brummer's frigate fought against another English frigate, but after a long battle "the *Two Esters* was compelled to strike to the enemy." Brummer was taken prisoner and joined to serve the English fleet.[136]

Jacob Wilhelm de Pont (1755-1809), a Swedish officer of French origin, was a lieutenant in the Swedish and then in the American navies. He served on the American frigate *Concord* and fought bravely but was captured by the English frigate *Blond*. Badly wounded, he was taken prisoner. Later released, he continued the war in the American fleet and was taken prisoner twice more before returning to Sweden.

Bengt Axel Gartman was a student at the University of Uppsala and entered the Swedish navy for the adventure. In 1778, he volunteered to serve in the French fleet. He was captured, but released, and joined the American fleet and served brilliantly under the famous command of Captain Johnson, participating in the celebrated White Haven raid.

Peter Holm (1758-1833), served in the Swedish navy and joined an American ship: "I immediately went to Gothenburg and took hire as gunner on an American ship called the *Delaware*. (*Ibid.,* p. 253). Off the coast of Philadelphia, there was a furious battle of 22 hours, in which the *Delaware* lost her captain and most of her crew. Holm was captured by the English warship *Reasonable*. He returned to Sweden in 1783 and re-entered the navy.

---

[135] Ibid., 181.
[136] Ibid., 203.

Johan Meijer (unknown dates), soldier of fortune and an officer in the Swedish army, was accepted as a *volontaire d'honneur* (honored volunteer) in the American service on the frigate *Ranger*. His commander was the famous Captain John Paul Jones. During a battle, Johan Meijer saved him and obtained very favorable recommendations for this. Later, Johan joined the French fleet and participated in the war in America.

The Sieges of Gibraltar (1779-83) and Minorca (1781-82)

Back in Europe, as an outcrop of what had become in fact a new global war, the French laid siege to Gibraltar. On 12 April 1779, the Treaty of Aranjuez allied Spain with France. This outcome was a long-term consequence of the victory in the War of the Spanish Succession, made possible by the family pact of the Bourbons, who now ruled both countries, albeit independently of each other. Spain had reasons other than family solidarity to enter the war. It wanted to regain its lost colonies of Florida, Minorca and, most importantly, Gibraltar – an issue down to our own day.[137] The English had taken it in 1704, and thereby commanded the junction of the Mediterranean Sea with the Atlantic Ocean. In the summer of 1799, its garrison was commanded by George Eliott, who was in an excellent position to threaten both French and Spanish shipping.

In early 1780, the United Provinces allied themselves to France and Spain. On 16 January, the British defeated the Spanish at the Battle of Cape Vincent, sometimes known as the Battle of the Moonlight, off the coast of Portugal, in which the young Horatio Nelson played a brilliant and valorous role. Spain then turned to France for reinforcements. Louis XVI responded by sending twelve warships under the command of de Guichen. He was to work in conjunction with the very aged and imperious Spanish Don Luis de Dordova y Cordova – 76 years old – who commanded the immense but unwieldy warship, *The Most Holy Trinity*.

A few months later, on 25 June 1781, twenty French warships commanded by Admiral de Guichen departed Brest and joined the Spanish

---

[137] Jean Le Michaud d'Arçon, *Histoire du siège de Gibraltar* (Cadix, 1783), p. 103; Raymond Sereau, *Un régiment de l'Ancien Régime, le Royal-Suédois et sa dernière campagne (Gibraltar 1782)*, (Paris, 1937), p. 27.

fleet, which was transporting troops towards Cartagena, on the Mediterranean coast of Spain. The two fleets maneuvered as best they could to deceive the enemy. The initial battle plan for Minorca was to disembark the principal force in the Bay of Mesquida and a secondary one in the Bay of Alcaufar, and to blockade two other important ports, Ciudadela and Fornells. It was then expected that Port-Mahon would be assaulted, with a force coming from Mesquida. The road to Georgetown and Fort St. Philip would then be blocked. A third force would disembark on the beaches of Degollador and Ciudadela. A detachment of men would also be sent to Fornell to capture its artillery.

On 19 August, the Duke de Crillon, the French captain-general, who was also Lieutenant General of the Royal Armies, arrived at Minorca and then at Cadiz, with some 105 ships. He was to command some 9,000 Spaniards, along with a further 3,000 men from the Lyonnais, Bretagne, and Bouillon Regiments. It soon became apparent that the British had implemented a serious defensive infrastructure of the island. Moreover, the weather worked against the attackers, with wind preventing their disembarkation at Ciudadela. The plans were therefore altered. Eventually, the French troops took up positions under the walls of the Fort St. Philip, under the command of General Murray.

The castle was protected by an immense rock. Its defensive moat was twenty feet deep and its walls sixty feet high. It was defended by a moderately sized British garrison that was well prepared, but not difficult to blockade by land and sea. Moreover, Don Carlos le Maire, marshal-general of logistics and chief of the engineers, along with Don Tortola, chief of the artillery and one of the great specialists in mines in Europe, succeeded in crossing the defensive trenches. An artillery battle then ensued, lasting until November.

On 23 October 1781, the Royal Swedish Regiment finally arrived. Fifty-two vessels, escorted by the frigates *La Sultana* and *La Flore* and the corvettes *La Badine* and *La Paulette* departed Toulon. They transported the body of troops led by Field Marshal Baron de Falkenhayn, whose ranks included the RSR.

In July, 1782, a joint Franco-Spanish expedition to Gibraltar included the RSR, which had concluded its operation at Fort Mahon. The French forces were definitely the weaker of the two, but altogether they amounted to a formidable 40,000 men and laid siege to the British fortress colony. Some 4,000 men were from the four regiments; Bretagne, Lyonnais, Bouillon and the RSR. The RSR was now commanded by Colonel Baron Hugues Hamilton. It included 56 officers, 947 men, 28 women, and 29 officers' servants, who were taken on board the *Sérieux, Pèlerin, Jeanne-Jacob, Jean-Baptiste*, and *Saint-Tropez*. Upon disembarking on Minorca, they took position in the trenches around Fort St. Philip. There they were confronted by an artillery assault. This great bombardment finally came to an end on 11 November, when hand-to-hand combat ensued. In a letter to the Marquis de Ségur, Baron Falkenhayn recounted that a soldier of the Lyonnais regiment lay side by side with one of the RSR. One had had his right leg amputated, the other his left. Having been given words of encouragement in their plight by the field marshal, the two men replied with wry humor, "Now we only need to buy one pair of shoes between us"".[138]

The Surrender of Minorca (1782)

After almost three years of siege, Fort St. Philip seemed impregnable to the Spanish. Responsibility for the operation gradually fell to the French. The Count de Vergennes refused to send the 40 vessels demanded by the Spanish, complaining, "The whole weight of the war falls on us alone and Spain seems to be taking part only as a spectator."[139] Louis XVI was increasingly weary of waging this war because of the funds it required, not so much in the Mediterranean but, from May 1781, in the Caribbean and Florida.

On 1 January 1782, Falkenhayn realized that when the Siege of Mahon ended he would need to move with his men to Gibraltar. Four officers of the RSR Infantry boarded the 110-gun *Royal-Louis*, which had participated in the American War of Independence. The infantry followed a few days later, assembling at Cadiz under the orders of the Chevalier de Beausset, Chief of the Squadron, and Admiral d'Estaing. Verdon de la

---

[138] Le Michaud d'Arçon, *Histoire du siège de Gibraltar*, p. 68.
[139] Henri Doniol, *Le comte de Vergennes et P.M. Hennin, 1749-1787* (Paris, 1898), p. 94.

Crêne was flag captain. From there they all proceeded to Gibraltar. Meanwhile, on 6 January, the bombardment of Fort St. Philip intensified but the assault failed.

From 15 to 20 January, the relationship among the British commanding officers deteriorated. Stores of meat were destroyed in a fire, and the men no longer had access to fresh commodities. Scurvy broke out. On 4-5 February Fort St. Philip surrendered, which opened the way for Fort Mahon to fall as well. The garrison – 1,200 soldiers, 250 artillerymen, 700 sailors, 900 men suffering from disease, and 200 Corsicans and Greeks – all became prisoners of war. Their resistance having been admirable, they were allowed to leave honorably, bearing their weapons, beating their tambours, torches illuminated and flags unfurled. The Duke de Crillon was made Duke de Mahon. French engineer Michaud d'Arçon commemorated them with an ode:

> The flag of peace floats on the debris.
> I go down; I see our ancient cohorts.
> A voice resounds: "Long live Charles and Louis!"
> Saint-Philippe surrenders and opens its doors to us.
> I mingle with the soldiers; I applaud their valor;
> I love my King, France, and give thanks for the honor.
> Bretagne, Lyonnais, Immortal Legions.
> And you, brave Germans, who from the icy lands of the North,
> Leaving your Sovereigns without being unfaithful to them,
> Come, under our flags, to give, to brave death,
> Be happy; Crillon gives you his vote;
> The smile of a Hero is the price of courage.[140]

From 20-23 May, the troops embarked with the rest of the fleet, commanded by Admiral Édouard-Thomas de Burgues, Count de Missiessy. On 27 May, they passed Cartagena and then Almeria, fighting the winds which blew against them until 3 June. They then enjoyed a stopover at Malaga from 10-16 June, before proceeding to Gibraltar, where they came into view on 17 May. On 18 May, the fleet arrived at San Roque and the troops disembarked three days later and installed themselves in the fields. The RSR spent July in the fields below Gibraltar

---

[140] Le Michaud d'Arçon, *Histoire du siège de Gibraltar*, p. 100.

there and set up their trenches. From the beginning, in 1779, the blockade had been a failure and pamphlets began to course through the ranks:

> To the Gentlemen of the Field at San Roque:
>
> Gentlemen of San Roque, between you and me,
> This is beyond a mockery.
> Are you going to take a whole lifetime
> Or will you actually finish one of these days?
> Can you not combine valor
> With the talent of keeping things short?
> Your eternal patience
> Does not tire of besieging;
> But you bring ours to an end.
> Be therefore defeaters or defeated,
> Gentlemen of the camp or of the blockade,
> End it one way or the other;
> Finish, for we can stand it no longer.
> Frequent are your cannonades;
> But alas! What have they produced?
> The quiet Englishman sleeps to the noise
> Of your nocturnal banging and crackling;
> Or if he answers from time to time
> To your prudent fury,
> It's out of consideration, I'll wager,
> And to say, 'I hear you.'
> Four years must have made you wise.
> So leave your old works where they are,
> Leave your old entrenchments,
> Withdraw, old besiegers:
> One day this memorable siege
> Will be ended by your children,
> If God will protect them.
> My friends, you can see it clearly,
> Your bombs bombard nothing;
> Your ships and your corvettes,
> And your works and your miners
> Only frighten the readers
> Of your formidable gazettes.
> Your blockade does not block,
> And thanks to your delightful skills,

Those whom you constantly starve
Will only perish from being overweight.[141]

From 14-20 July, the RSR took to the trenches. Then, in August, the Spanish, unable to take the initiative, relinquished their responsibilities to the French. Louis XVI demanded a final major assault. The engineer Le Michaud d'Arçon was put in charge. Urgency was necessary since it had become apparent that a British fleet was coming to Gibraltar's aid under the command of Admiral Howe.

From 9-14 August, the RSR remounted their trenches and extended them a further 701 meters towards the enemy. With respect to them:

> How the French division would serve had not yet been settled. It was decided that being roughly the sixth part of the combined army, it would be the sixth in general service, and would guard the lines every six days. It was ordered that each battalion, starting with the first of the Lyonnais, would be intended for the guard of the first line, and that the grenadiers and chasseurs of the other regiments, supported by 200 fusiliers of each, would go to the second line, would bivouac under the orders of the lieutenant-colonel of the trench regiment and would retire in the morning to the forts of the first line where they would spend the day, but that the 600 men of auxiliary pickets would return to the camp to do the interior service there: the lines being always commanded at night by a brigadier and a colonel; it was ruled that a brigadier would march whenever the French would be of service. The colonel of the regiment who supplied the trench battalion had to be the second in command during the night and in chief during the day, because the brigadier retired in the morning and one brigadier per regiment was required. The Marquis de Bouzols, made marshal of the camp after the Mahon campaign, and appointed our second general, offered to serve as brigadier and marched when his old regiment was mounting the trenches. The Comte de Sparre, Camp Master in command of the Royal Swedish regiment, was appointed to march with the Bretagne, the Marquis de Crillon with the Royal Swedish, and the Comte de Crillon with the Bouillon.[142]

On 3 July, the French army marched to the line, a service it continued to perform until October 16.

The French regiments were striking in their appearance:

---

[141] Ibid., 100.
[142] Ibid.

> The days when we had to march were days of great curiosity for the Spaniards. General and subaltern officers, soldiers, all flocked to our camp; all wanted to see us, all looked at us with that astonishment which proves their inferiority. The beauty of our regiments, the ensemble and the rapidity of our movements, our military music, were new objects for them. It can be assured that the peoples of America did not admire the Spanish troops any more than they admired us. I am not afraid to say, indeed, that the four regiments employed in Menorca and Gibraltar, without being the finest in the French army, were nevertheless very well composed, superiorly kept and that they maneuvered perfectly. This was the homage which Murray paid to them, when they were presented to him ... It may be presumed here that the stay of this division in the camp of Saint-Roch and in Cadiz will bring about a revolution in the Spanish army. Nations are enlightened only by communication. The troops are in Spain two centuries away from the troops of France and Prussia. It is after having seen French regiments that the Spanish regiments will acquire that taste for cleanliness which is the ornament of the man of war, and what is even more precious, the preservation of health: it is by imitating us that the legions, so famous in the past, will be initiated into the mysteries of tactics, and will again become the glory of their country.[143]

In gale force winds, which actually helped to make them more difficult to be spotted, some 1,200 men carried out their work on the night of 15-16 August. The following day, the king's brother, the Count d'Artois, and the Duke de Bourbon arrived at San Roque. They were amazed to see that in only four hours the previous night, similar trenches had been constructed along the whole length, 8- 9 feet by 10 feet thick, and that the lines of communication were six feet high along their entire length. The men continued construction the following night, but were confronted by two heavy British barrages. On 2 September, the RSR mounted their line to relieve the Bretagne Regiment. Finally, on 6 September the new trenches were completed. Some 190 cannon, and mortars were prepared along the line. The assault now was imminent. Michaud d'Arçon described the preparations for the battle:

> Everything was in motion in Algeciras and on the sea; everything was in operation in the camps, in the arsenals, in stores, all workshops. In the forest, which is three leagues from Saint-Roch, fascines were made which the horses of the cavalry and the dragoons went to fetch and

---

[143] Ibid.

carried to the artillery park. Vessels loaded with ammunition of all kinds arrived every day. The seashores were covered with men unloading cannons, mortars, carriages. In the parks you could see huge piles of cannonballs and bombs being raised; in the parks one could see enormous piles of cannonballs and bombs being raised; under the sheds far from the camp the devices which ignite the bombs and cause them to explode were being composed; in the arsenals they were forging day and night; the main roads of the camp were covered with wagons filled with munitions of war and of mouth. Military instruments were heard on all sides, everywhere we saw regiments in battle, detachments on the march, and in the midst of this multitude of active beings, the Duke de Crillon was the sublime engine, the man of genius who decides.[144]

The Prince of Nassau, major general of the expeditions, decided to board one of his prams, the *Talla-Piedra*. A certain O'Connell, lieutenant colonel of the RSR; Armfeldt, a captain of the RSR; and d'Arçon were all there, too.

On 8 September, the battle commenced in earnest. The British bombardment totally destroyed the Mahon redoubt. In his report, Falkenhayn mentioned those who participated from the RSR: "Monsieur de Montaigne, Second Captain; Rousseau, Second Lieutenant of the Grenadiers; de Gallmberg, Second Captain, de Queffen, Sub-lieutenant of the Chasseurs; de Nioldarm, Captain Commanding; de Montfort and de la Flotte, Sub-lieutenants of the fusiliers."[145]

The French cannon fired on the fort, with the Count d'Artois and Duke de Bourbon in attendance.

On 11 September, Le Michaud d'Arçon recorded:

Each regiment provided 100 men commanded by a captain and a lieutenant or second lieutenant, a choice of the commanding camp masters. This detachment of 400 men was commanded by Mr. O'Connell charged by the general with this important commission. Allow me to name here the French officers who had the honour of being chosen by the heads of the regiments, and who had such a glorious part in the dangers of this memorable expedition. Messieurs de Blaton and Gatines, from the Lyonnais; Messieurs du Bérard and Siscé, from the Bretagne; Messieurs Baron of Armfeld and Myring, of the Royal-Swedish; Messieurs de Klie and de la Tour, from the Bouillon, were those of our

---

[144] Ibid.
[145] Sereau, *Le Royal-Suédois*, p. 17.

comrades who were entrusted with the command of each detachment provided by each regiment.

That evening, some regiments were dining happily, "still dining when the detachments went into battle."[146]

On 12 September, having cut the route of Admiral Howe who was coming to relieve the defenders, the Franco-Spanish fleet arrived at Gibraltar. It counted 39 ships of the line, eighteen of which were French. They were commanded by Don Luis de Cordoba. Another eleven ships were in the adjacent Bay of Algeciras. On 13 September, the men of the RSR, with other forces, approached the British-held fort. The regiment also provided five officers and 300 men, who boarded two ships. De Puységur wrote:

> Let us imagine the importance of this day, the result of which was to be the surrender of the strongest place known, on which the whole of Europe had its eyes open. Let us imagine the honorable consequences of a success for the attackers, the glory of victory before the eyes of the brother and nephew of their kings, and we will have an idea of the value of the troops, of the will of the leaders, of the state of fear and hope in which the two combined armies of land and sea found themselves, whose eyes were all fixed on the march of the prams.[147]

The prams soon approached the fort, supported by 48 vessels of the Franco-Spanish Fleet. Each pram carried 200 men and forty 24-inch guns. The British were fully aware of this activity and also that relations between the French and Spanish were poor. Elliot flooded the galleries on the flank of the rock below the fort, while opening a powerful artillery barrage.

According to Michaud d'Arçon, who sailed with the attacking fleet, the departure was hasty and poorly prepared because many of the batteries hit the bottom of the rock before they had even been properly put in position.[148] Only two of the prams were able to position themselves properly, namely, *La Pastora* and *La Talla-Piedra*, the latter commanded by the Prince of Nassau. They were stationed before the most formidable battery, the Bastion Royal. Covering fire was nonexistent. Nonetheless,

---

[146] Le Michaud d'Arçon, op. cit.
[147] Sereau, *Le Royal-Suédois*, p. 75.
[148] Le Michaud d'Arçon, *Histoire du siège de Gibraltar*, op. cit.

the prams in action proved devastating to the British. On board the *Talla Piedra*, joy reigned; the men were delighted to hear the cannonballs hit massive structural parapets. The inventor was congratulated and embraced. All were enthusiastic to see the walls of Gibraltar breached.[149]

After two hours, the Prince of Nassau reported to the Count d'Artois that the danger was great, and that he had lost sixty killed and wounded in less than half an hour. But his pram was holding up well, the cannonballs were easily extinguished, and he hoped to breach the entrance to Gibraltar soon.[150] Shortly thereafter, the situation deteriorated: on the *Talla-Piedra*, the gunpowder had to be doused with water, as it was in danger of exploding. Lieutenant-Colonel O'Connell was wounded in the head and arm. Michaud d'Arçon, seeing that his troops were alone to sustain the fight, said sadly, "We are abandoned by God and men."[151]

At 6 p.m., O'Connell reported to the Count d'Artois, despite having been wounded twice in the assault. Five hours later, the occupants of the remaining prams fled. Captain d'Armfeldt "embarked in the last boat, persisting, in spite of the urgings of his soldiers, in not wanting to leave the battery until the very last moment, though it was almost entirely on fire."[152]

In the flight back from Gibraltar, many of the wounded were carried away in French and Spanish boats but many, too, were saved by the British defenders. Lieutenant de Myrin, of the RSR, however, had had his thigh blown away and was one of the mortal casualties. Michaud d'Arçon echoed this failure while explaining its causes: "All the gunboats and bombards which accomplished nothing on the 13th and 14th had been badly built and almost all were badly controlled: too small to hold the sea, not in heavy weather, but when the surface was rippled by the gentlest wind. They could not be employed as needs required. ... 60 bad ones were built; only 40 good ones needed to be built, which could have sailed when the service required."[153]

The Chevalier de Cotignon analyzed it thus:

---

[149] Sereau, *Le Royal-Suédois*, op. cit., p. 16.
[150] Ibid.
[151] Ibid., 18.
[152] Ibid., 18.
[153] Le Michaud d'Arçon, *op.cit.*

Each pram had powder to fire for two days. Imagine the explosion! In an instant men, arms and heads were seen in the air ... The explosion of these prams had been heard from Cadiz, albeit twenty leagues away, but it was heard from much further afield. The shock was so strong that there was not a single pane of glass left, both in Gibraltar and in Algeciras, and the inhabitants felt like an earthquake had hit. As for us, we were deaf for several days.[154]

Those who fought with distinction were rewarded, despite the failure of the assault. A few days later, "the Count d'Artois granted a pension of 600 livres from his coffer, and sent 150 to the four sergeants who had distinguished themselves the most during the action: there was one from each regiment. François Pradon, from the Lyonnais; Mathieu Noël, known as Mouchi, from the Bretagne; Christian Matthies, from the Royal-Suédois; Antoine Mayer, from the Bouillon, were those to whom the prince granted this honorable grace; and this time at least, the merit of obscure men was not without reward and did not remain unknown."[155]

This largesse was at least partially recouped when a British ship carrying money and official letters for the Gibraltar officers was intercepted. The Duke de Crillon asked Lieutenant O'Connell of the RSR to translate them. "A lot of money was found there which the Jews in Gibraltar sent to their correspondents in Livorno. Governor Elliot's letters had been thrown into the sea; but they had forgotten to throw in them those of the officers of the garrison, which were seized by the Spaniards and brought to the Duke of Crillon, who had them interpreted by M. O'Connell, an Irishman, lieutenant-colonel of the Royal Swedish. They all attested to the anxieties of the besieged, and the fears inspired by the bravery of their governor, who was determined to defend to the last drop of his blood."[156]

On 20 September, M. de la Motte-Picquet, on *L'Invincible,* gave chase to the Howe's squadron, which had fled from Gibraltar after being attacked. On 11 October a brief engagement finally took place between the two by Cape Spartel. Howe's squadron included some 38 ships of the line and succeeded in evading the 183 French and Spanish transport ships.

---

[154] Sereau, *Le Royal-Suédois*, op. cit.
[155] Ibid.
[156] Ibid.

On 11 November, Walther von Nyvenheim became commander of the RSR.

Further campaigns of the Royal Swedish Regiment

As the American War of Independence wound down, the French squadron returned to Cadiz. Thereafter, soldiers under the flag of France, many of whom had been serving for five years, dispersed. The Treaty of Paris, signed on 3 September, officially ended the war. The RSR, still based at San Roque, returned to France to be garrisoned at Avesnes, near Calais.

On 21 September, the regiment was officially purchased by Count Axel von Fersen assisted by both his own King Gustaf III and Queen Marie Antoinette. The latter's involvement led to considerable gossip at Versailles. As Fersen wrote Gustaf, "the King consented immediately and showed the greatest desire to do something that would be agreeable to Your Majesty. The Queen was willing to get involved as soon as she knew that you wanted to."[157]

In October, the Second Battalion of the RSR was transferred to Philippeville, where it remained until 1785. Its former owner Colonel Ludwig Ernst Joseph Sparre, Count von Kronenberg, now received two pensions of 12,000 and 6000 lives each for his role in the campaigns of 1782-83, especially after he became Field Marshal of the Royal Armies.[158] A ceremony took place, in front of the troops. Kronenberg described the departure of Sparre and the arrival of Fersen thus in a lengthy narration:

> The King has granted the Count of Fersen, a young Swedish lord, the property of the Royal Swedish regiment, in place of the Count of Sparre, who has been made Marshal of Camp, and who is retired with a pension. This officer, on leaving his regiment, addressed the following letter to his officers:
>
> Gentlemen, born among you, raised your comrade and become your leader, if any consolation can soften my regrets in losing the honor of commanding you, it is to think that you will find in my successor all the feelings that I have devoted to you, and the name of Fersen is your guarantee of this. His Majesty the King of Sweden wanted your corps to

---

[157] Françoise Kermina, *Fersen* (Perrin, 2001), p. 254.
[158] Ibid., p. 254.

be commanded by a Swede (request of October 30, 1742), who had only one homeland; I had two, due to events which the kindnesses of the French court will never allow me to complain about. I dare to hope that until my last breath no one will serve my new homeland with a purer and more ardent zeal. But Sweden will be dear to me forever. Filled at all times, and particularly at this moment, with the kindness of her King, that all her subjects will always regard me as their compatriot, that the brave officers who will fight under the banners of the regiment, will always regard me as their comrade, and that all those who will come to Paris will always see my house as their own. You know, Gentlemen, the feelings of attachment that we have devoted to you, Madame de Sparre and I: glory and favor will follow your new leader everywhere, and my heart will always be in your midst; it will always appreciate your successes. Love me, my friends, and in lamenting the happiness of living with you, never forget the feelings I had for you and the rights that the Sparres have always wanted to acquire in your friendship.

The officers responded to their former colonel with the following letter:

M. le Comte, charged by the corps of officers of the Royal-Swedish regiment to reply in its name to the letter which you have done it the honor of writing to it, charged with sending you the general expression of its regrets, we must assure you, Monsieur le Comte, that we were all as sorry to lose you as touched by the obliging testimonies of esteem, friendship and remembrance with which your letter is full. Each of us in particular, and all of us in general, renew to you the assurance of our gratitude for the obligations which bind us to you; Monsieur le Comte, it will never fade from our grateful and sensitive hearts, nor will the memory of a family, whose name has always been dear and glorious to the Royal Swedish regiment.

Being one and the same family, and considering ourselves as equally attached by the most ardent zeal to the service of His Most Christian Majesty the King of France; and by the most lively gratitude to His Majesty the King of Sweden, to whose protection his continual attention to the regiment assures us of precious rights; we are convinced, M. le Comte, that you have not failed to recommend us equally to your successor, Count de Fersen, without any distinction of country or nation, since we are all animated by the same spirit, as if we had only one country.

We have only one heart and one voice, M. le Comte, to assure you of our regrets, of the eternal memory which we preserve of your kindnesses, and of the respect with which we will never cease to be, M. le Comte, etc. Signed on behalf of the corps, Baron de Sparre, captain; the knight of the Everlanges; Witri, lieutenant; Schiomaire the elder, second lieutenant.[159]

In 1784, Alexander de Sparre was promoted to lieutenant-general and awarded the Great Cross of the Sword. Already in January of that year, the RSR had been transferred to Landrecies and Valenciennes, where its troops remained until March 1787. Command was given over to Curt von Stedingk, who remained in this post until 1791.

On 24 February 1791, Baron de Fock, a Swede who had been Lauzun's aide-de-camp in America, wrote Washington asking that he and Axel von Fersen be received into the Order of the Cincinnati. Meanwhile, in March, the younger Fersen returned from Sweden and took official possession of the RSR. From January 1786, he divided his time between the French court at Versailles and Landrecies and Valenciennes, where the regiment was stationed. Later in the year, after spending 2-10 June at Valenciennes with the RSR, he returned to Sweden on 25 June.

In 1787, with a new Anglo-French crisis looming, French military forces were once again reorganized into divisions. The RSR was sent to Maubeuge. There, from 15-20 May, Fersen inspected his regiment before departing once again for Versailles. He repeated this pattern again on 23 June. However, from 5-18 October, he succeeded in having the RSR transferred back to Valenciennes. He then returned to Versailles before, once again, departing for Sweden.

---

[159] *Mercure historique et politique de Bruxelles*, Vol. 18, p. 126, 127, 128.

Chapter 6:

The French Revolution and the End of the Royal Swedish Regiment

Revolutionary Disturbances Commence

From March 1789, the RSR was garrisoned at Valenciennes, where they were when the Estates General convened on 5 May. Louis XVI had summoned that ancient body, which had not met for 175 years, after multiple failed attempts through other means to address France's mounting fiscal crisis. In June, Fersen left Versailles to rejoin his regiment. In July, Marshal de Broglie decided to send the Royal Swedes back to Versailles but reversed the order at the last minute.

On 24 September, Fersen officially settled in Versailles, but in early October his regiment returned to Valenciennes. On 6 October, he witnessed the radical march on Versailles, which ended with the Royal Family's forced move to Paris. On 29 December, Fersen rejoined his regiment at Valenciennes, only to depart for Aix-la-Chapelle (today Aachen, in Germany), where Gustaf III's orders awaited him as a secret agent to assist the Royal Family.

Fersen and the Flight of the Royal Family to Varennes

Fersen monitored the situation carefully, as Louis XVI tried to balance revolutionary fervor with his precarious position on a throne with limited powers. In 1791, however, he attempted to flee the country in disguise to rally foreign forces to crush the revolution. This was unsuccessful, as the party was stopped at Varennes and forced to return to Paris under military escort. According to Antoine Henri de Jomini, Sweden played a role, calling it "a concerted project with the King of Sweden for the flight of Louis."[160] Gustaf III's proximity appears to have played a role, for the "plan seemed to be connected with the arrival of the King of Sweden on the banks of the Rhine. Either this Monarch had really consulted with Catherine, the French princes or the secret ministers of Louis, or he wished to aspire to the glory of re-establishing royal authority in France, as he had done in his own country, he had gone to Belgium in the month of May 1791, on the pretext of taking the waters of Spa for the wounds received in the Finnish war."[161]

"Gustaf III's plan," in other words:

> was to put himself at the head of the emigrants, the Royal Swedish regiment, and the French troops who had remained faithful, and to restore Louis XVI to the full extent of his authority: in order to make his success more certain, the King was to join him in rallying all the discontented of the kingdom. This combination of circumstances made many people think that this singular enterprise was the result of the secret powers given to M. de Bréteuil, and it was believed to be proved by the attention of the King's advisers to put a prince who was naturally a friend and ally of France at the head of the expedition, so as not to leave the direction of the war to a rival power, such as Prussia or Austria. This calculation, which would honor their intentions, did little to their diplomatic judgement; for a civil war was always a calamity which would tear France apart, and from which too many jealous and powerful neighbors were interested in taking advantage. Moreover, it was a gross error to imagine that the revolution would have ended with the presence of 50,000 men under Paris. This would have been at most to be hoped for in 1789, but in the two years that the parties had been in conflict they had had time to deploy their forces, and one does not subjugate a country in turmoil with a handful of men.[162]

Meanwhile, the RSR continued to function. Its command was now transferred to Charles-Léopold Fürstenwärther. Yet subjects of the Swedish king, including Aminoff, Armfeldt, Gallenberg, Gedda, Hopken, and Reutersverd, among others, remained active. According to a royal

---

[160] Antoine Henri de Jomini, *Histoire critique et militaire des guerres de la Révolution: rédigée sur de nouveaux documents, et augmentée d'un grand nombre de cartes et de plans* (Paris, 1820).
[161] Ibid.
[162] Ibid.

decree of 1 January 1790, in the wake of Louis XVI's reclusion in the Tuileries, all infantry regiments, including the RSR, changed their "royal" appellations. Only the Swiss Guards were allowed to retain theirs. In consequence, the RSR was combined with the 14th Light Infantry Regiment to form the 89th Infantry Regiment.

The end of the Royal Swedish Regiment

The failure of Louis XVI's flight reduced Gustaf III's plans to naught. Their fellow monarchs, friend and foe, united in horror at the revolutionary events in France. As the French monarchy receded in power and approached its end, the illustrious role of the RSR in France also approached its conclusion.

On 14 December 1791, an Army of the North was created and placed under Marshal de Rochambeau, who commanded it until 1792. Its purpose was to defend France against the allied forces arrayed against it, whose purpose was to crush the revolution and return France to its former system. Under its new name, the 89th Infantry Regiment, the RSR formed a unit within the new Army.

On 11 February 1792, the vestiges of the RSR, now within the 89th Infantry, comprised 1,354 men on paper, but 161 had dropped out. On the same day, Fersen, who had returned from Sweden, decided to rejoin Marie-Antoinette in Paris but first visited the 89th, incognito together with his adjutant Baron Reuterswärd. On 20 April, the National Assembly, together with Louis XVI under duress, declared war on Austria, now ruled by Marie Antoinette's nephew Francis II.

The French army was ill prepared. Many officers resigned, deserted, or led without enthusiasm. The 1st Battalion of the 89th Regiment – which contained the RSR – was reassigned to the Army of the Moselle, while the 2nd Battalion remained with the Army of the North. Colonel O'Connell, formerly of the RSR, was repeatedly pressed by General Dumouriez and war minister Carnot to accept a command. However, he declined and joined the Irish Brigade, garrisoned at Koblenz, a leading center of anti-revolutionary French émigrés. This brigade joined the forces of Karl Wilhelm, Duke of Brunswick, whose army consisted of 112,000 men, assembled from a variety of German states.

The RSR fell in the crossfire of the propaganda war. Louis-Marie Prudhomme's radical journal *Révolutions de Paris* attacked the monarchy and monarchists. He also attacked the foreign regiments, such as the former RSR, because they were ultimately commanded by foreign monarchs, some of whom had fought wars against France. As he wrote:

> we can no longer hide the fact that the army has not been the same for a year ... ten regiments went to the villainy of protecting the flight of the king, when it was still useful to retain it in France, and Royal German, and Royal Liège, and Royal Swedish, and all the foreign troops, and the Swiss guard; dare we say that these regiments are animated by the same spirit as our National Guards? And what a difference there is between the discipline that is imposed in these corps and that which has been established in the volunteer battalions. The latter have chosen their officers, count their leaders only by the number of their friends, obey only the law, and because they want to obey it, whereas in the troops of the line, and especially in the foreign troops, the officers have still retained all the arrogance and all the insolence of the old government. The line army regime is a regime of injustice and oppression; the Constituent Assembly sacrificed the rights of soldiers to the glory of the officers it held in its midst; our line soldiers are nothing but war machines, subject to all the bizarre whims of ancient feudalism; and how can we expect men who have made no other commitment than to go and die in defense of the fatherland to submit to the arbitrariness of these uncertain and despotic wills?[163]

On 27 April, the flag of the 89th Regiment was blessed, along with that of the Nation Guard. The old flag of the Royal Swedish Regiment was then publicly burned in the presence of both the military and civil notables of Valenciennes. The regiment then rejoined the Army of the North. Its first military action took place en route, at Quiévrain. The regiment's relationship with the Army of the North was poor, however, a situation aggravated by the attempt of two officers to go over to the allies on 7 June. On 25 June, the regiment was positioned at the center of the 1st Infantry Division, under the command of Field Marshal Isidore de Lynch, an Irish officer.

On 13 June, the Prussians, who had also come into the war, invaded France and took Longwy. The Marquis de Bouillé, who had organized the

---

[163] Louis-Marie Prudhomme, *Révolutions de Paris: dédiées à la nation et au district des Petits Augustins*, Volume 11, p. 166.

failed flight of the Royal Family to Varennes, was now in the army of Louis-Joseph de Bourbon, Prince of Condé. He would shortly flee to England, where he died on 14 November 1800. On 25 July, the Duke of Brunswick issued a manifesto to the people of Paris, warning them that the security of the Royal Family was under threat and that he would take reprisals against the city if harm befell them. His rhetoric inflamed the revolutionary mob. On 10 August, they invaded the Tuileries, where they had resided since their removal from Versailles. The loyal Swiss Guards defending them were massacred, and the Royal Family fled to the mercy of the Legislative Assembly, then the elected body constituting government. The foreign armies continued to close in, but on 20 September they were stopped at Valmy.

In a position of strength, the following day, 21 September, the French monarchy was abolished and replaced by a republic. Government was turned over to a National Convention, which held a democratic constitution in abeyance while carrying out authoritarian policies. These included the Reign of Terror, which witnessed massacres of suspected political opponents, military measures against recalcitrant regions, and show trials. After a trial by the Convention itself, on 21 January 1793, King Louis XVI was executed. France then declared war on Britain and the Netherlands. On 16 October, Queen Marie Antoinette was also executed. Fersen, who was rumored to have had an affair with her, wrote his sister:

> I have now lost everything I had in the world. Only you remain. She for whom I lived, who made me happy, for whom I lived, yes my dear Sophie, I never stopped loving her and would have sacrificed everything for her. She whom I loved so much, for whom I gave a thousand times my life, no longer exists ... I will always have her image in front of my eyes, in me, the memory of what she was for me will make me cry forever. Everything is over for me. Why couldn't I die by her side, shed my blood for her, for them?[164]

To his mistress Eléonore Sullivan, his mistress, Fersen despaired "that [the Queen] was alone in her last moments, without consolation, without anyone to talk to and to whom she could have expressed her wishes, is

---

[164] Kermina, *Fersen*, p. 284.

dreadful. What henchmen of Satan! No, if I don't get my revenge, my soul will never be at peace."[165]

The former Royal Swedes remained split between the 1st Battalion of the 89th Regiment with the Army of the North, and the 2nd Battalion with the Army of Sambre-et-Meuse. On 6 April, the 2nd Battalion was attached the 162nd Demi-Brigade at Bergues. Then, on 19 July, the 1st Battalion was assigned to 161st Demi-Brigade.

Two years later, in 1796, a further amalgamation of battalions took place, but by then the Royal Swedish Regiment had lost any independent identity within the French army and ceased to exist.

---

[165] Ibid., 285.

Index

A

Aix-la-Chapelle (Aachen, Deutschland), 105
Alcaufar (bay of, Minorca), 91
Alliance (Quadruple), 25, 26
Algeciras (Spain), 96, 98, 100
Alheim (Jean-Baptiste, Baron of Limosin d', Captain in RSR), 40
Allen (battle of, Deutschland), 41
Almeria (Spain), 93
Alsace, 3, 19, 26, 28, 32, 36, 42, 44, 45
Alsace (French regiment of), 95, 96
Amblimont (Claude-Marguerite Renart de Fuchsamberg, Count of), 85
American Revolution (American, Independence war), 44, 67, 84, 87, 88, 92, 101
Aminoff (Carl Fredrik, Lieutenant in RSR), 43, 106
Anhalt (French regiment of), 44
Ancien Régime (Old Regime), 1, 4, 90
Andernach (siege of, Netherlands), 16
Andrews (Second-lieutenant in Sparre Regiment), 17
Angerville (Barthélemy-François-Joseph, Mouffle d'), 41
Annapolis (Maryland), 78
Ans (Belgium), 34
Anterroches (Joseph Charles Alexandre, Colonel, Count of), 29
Antilles (the), 76
Appelgrehn (Pierre, Swedish officer in Sparre regiment and Colonel), 27, 28, 31
Aranjuez (Treaty of), 90
Argenson (René Louis de Voyer de Paulmy, Marquis of), 30, 34, 35, 39
Argyll (Duke of), 21
Arleux (siege of), 23
Armfeldt (Carl Gustav d', Lieutenant then Captain in RSR), 43, 97, 99, 106
Arnold (Benedict), 71
Arneth (Alfred von), 69
Artois (Charles, Count of), 96, 97, 99, 100
Assas (Louis, Captain, nicknamed 'le chevalier de'), 1
Augenheim (Deutschland), 32
Augsburg (League of), 5, 6
Augustus II (Frédéric, King of Poland), 27
Austria, 1, 3, 4, 5, 14, 15, 23, 24, 27, 28, 29, 30, 31, 32, 33, 34, 39, 40, 42, 69, 106, 107
Austria (Maria-Theresa of, Queen of France), 14
Austrian Succession (War of), 29, 39, 42
Auxonne (French regiment of), 70
Avesnes (France), 68, 101

B

Baden (Great Duchy of), 18
Badine (the, French corvette), 91
Baltimore, 84

Barcelona (Siege of, Catalonia), 11, 12, 13
Barras (Jacques-Melchior de Saint-Laurent, Count of), 78
Barrau (Théodore-Henri), 28
Bassardrie (Joseph Alexandre Le Vaillant de la), 17
Bavaria (Electorate of), 15, 16, 19, 30, 32, 33, 42
Bavarian (French regiment of), 19, 30, 44
Beauce (French regiment of), 36
Beausset (Antoine Hilarion, Knight of), 92
Beckmann (Marareta), 6, 9, 12
Belgium, 5, 9, 34, 106
Belle-Isle (Charles Louis Auguste Fouquet, Duke of, Marshal of France), 27, 28, 29, 30, 32
Bérard (Monsieur du, officer, French regiment of Bretagne), 97
Bergen (battle of, Deutschland), 42, 38
Bergues (France), 110
Bernadotte, 43
Bernard (Jacques), 35
Bernier (Nicolas, French composer), 14
Berthier (Louis-Alexandre, Marshal of France), 77
Berwick (Jacques Fitz-James, Marshal of), 26, 27, 40
Bielefeld (Deutschland), 40
Bielke (Nils, Count), 6
Blamont (François Colin de, French composer), 28, 33, 40
Blaton (Monsieur de, officer, French regiment of Lyonnais), 97
Bled (Jean-Paul), 29
Blenheim (battle of, Belgium), 17
Blond (the, English frigate), 89
Bohemia, 30, 32, 40
Bois (Jean-Pierre), 24, 30
Bonald (Louis-Gabriel Ambroise de, Viscount of), 2

Boston (Massachusetts), 78, 85, 86, 88
Bouchain (France), 24
Boufflers (Duke of, Marshal of France), 15, 20, 21, 22
Bouillé (François Claude, Marquis of), 108
Bouillon (French regiment of), 91, 92, 95, 97, 100
Bourbon (House of), 1, 14, 25, 90
Bourbon-Condé (House of), 34
Bourbon-Condé (Louis III, Prince of), 40, 41
Bourbon-Condé (Louis V Joseph, Prince of), 96, 97, 109
Bourbonnais (French regiment of), 70
Bourgerie (Raymond), 81
Bouzols (Anne-Joachim de Montaigu, Marquis of), 95
Brace (the, French ship), 85
Brandywine (battle of), 67
Brest (French), 90
Bretagne (french regiment of), 91, 92, 93, 95, 96, 97, 100
Breteuil (Louis Auguste Le Tonnelier, Baron of), 106
Breuil (C,T, Sieur du), 37
Broglie (Victor-François, Duke of, Marshal of France), 29, 30, 31, 32, 41, 42, 43, 44, 68, 105
Brossard (Sébastien de, French composer), 14
Bruges, 20
Brummer (Johan Magnus), 89
Brunswick-Lunebourg (Ferdinand, Duke of), 41, 107, 109
Bülow (August Christian von), 43
Burgues (Edouard Thomas of, Count of Missiessy), 93
Byron (John, Rear admiral), 88

C

Cadiz, 91, 92, 96, 100, 101
Calais (France), 68, 101
Camden (battle of), 72, 88

Camisards (war of), 15, 17
Canada, 39, 88
Capes (battle of), 78
Cape Vincent (battle of, Portugal), 90
Caribbean, 83
Carleton (Guy, 1st Baron of), 84
Carlos le Maire (Don), 91
Carnot (Lazare Nicolas Marguerite), 107
Cartagena (Spain), 91, 93
Castelfollit (Siege of, Catalonia), 11
Cellamare (Conspiracy of), 26
Charleroi (Belgium), 19, 34
Charles II (King of Spain), 14
Charles V (Holy Roman Emperor), 23, 29
Charles VI (Holy Roman Emperor), 23, 24, 27
Charles VII (Holy Roman Emperor), 30
Charleston (South Carolina), 81, 85, 86
Chastellux (François Jean, Marquis of), 84
Chessapeake (bay of), 74, 76, 77, 78, 84
Catherine II of Russia, 105
Chevert (François de, French general), 1, 32, 40, 42
Chevrier (François-Antoine), 29
Choiseul (Etienne-François, Marquis de Stainville et Duc de), 3
Cincinnati (Society of the), 87, 88, 103
Ciudadela (port of, Minorca), 91
Clermont (Louis de Bourbon-Condé, Count of), 40, 41
Clinton (Henry, English general), 77, 79, 81
Coigny (François de Franquetot, Duke of, Marshal of France), 32
Colin (Jean-Albert-Alphonse), 37
Cologne (Electorate of), 5, 15, 40
Compiègne (France), 45
Concord (American frigate), 89

Condé (French House of), 34, 40, 41, 109
Contades (Louis Georges Ersame de, Marshal of), 41
Constituent Assembly, 108
Conti (Louis-François de Bourbon, Prince of), 34
Corbach (battle of), 43
Córdova (Luis de Córdova y, Spanish admiral), 90
Cornwallis (Charles, Marquis), 74, 75, 76, 78, 79, 80, 81
Cotignon (Jean-Jacques, Knight of), 99
Courland (Duchy of, Duke of), 24
Courten (Swiss regiment of, in the service of France), 30
Coste (Jean-François), 76
Crêne (Verdon de la, French flag captain), 93
Crillon (Louis des Balbes de Berton of, Duke of Mahon), 91, 93, 95, 97, 100
Creutz (Gustaf Philip, Count of), 46, 73, 81
Crompond (camp of), 85
Cumberland (William Augustus, Duke of), 36
Curaçao (Caribbean), 87
Custine (Adam Philippe de), 77

D

Degollador (Minorca), 91
Dahlstierna (Lieutenant in RSR), 40
Delaware (river), 85, 86
Delaware (American ship), 89
Denain (battle of, Belgium), 16, 24
Dettingen (battle of), 32
Dillon (Robert Guillaume), 72
Donauwörth (Deutschland), 32, 33
Doniol (Henri), 92
Douai, 20, 24
Drevon (Henry), 31
Dumas (Mathieu, French general), 69, 81

Dumouriez (Charles François du Perrier), 107
Dunkirk, 39
Dutch War, 5

E

Eckeren, Ekeren (battle of, Belgium), 16
Egra (Bohemia), 29, 30, 31, 32
Eisenach (Deutschland), 43
Ekeblad (Claes, Count of), 35
Elbhecq (Pierre Joseph du Chambge, Baron of, Major of the RSR), 45
Elgenstierna (Captain in RSR), 43
El Hage (Fadi, historian), 16, 21, 24
Eliott (George Augustus, Baron, English general), 90
Erskin (Carl-Gustaf, Baron), 6
Erskin (Regiment of), 6
Ettelingen (Captain in RSR), 34
Estaing (Charles Henri, Count of), 92
Estrées (Gabrielle, Marquise of), 11
Everlange de Witry (Robert-Joseph, called 'Knight of Witry', Lieutenant in RSR), 103

F

Falkenhayn (Charles Gustaf, baron of), 30, 91, 92, 97
Fersen (Hans Axel, Count of), 25, 46
Fersen (Fredrik Axel, Count of), 30, 35, 46
Fieffé (Eugène), 4
Flanders (province), 15, 17, 18, 19, 20, 21
Flemming (Baron of), 28
Fleurus (battle of), 5, 6
Fleury (André Hercule, Cardinal of), 27, 29
Flore (the, French ship), 91
Florida, 88, 90, 92
Flotte (Monsieur de, Sub-Lieutenant of the Fusiliers in RSR), 97
Fock (Johan Henrik, Baron of), 87, 88, 103

Folard (Jean-Charles, Chevalier de), 26, 37, 45
Fontarabie (Spain), 26
Fontenoy (battle of), 29, 30
Fornells (port of, Minorca), 91
Fourteenth Light Infantry Regiment, 107
Franklin (Benjamin), 68
French Revolution, 2, 105
Frederik I (King of Sweden), 28
Frederik II (King of Prussia, 'the Great'), 29, 31, 33, 37, 39
Frederik V (King of Denmark), 38
Freiburg im Breisgau, 32
Friedberg (Deutschland), 41, 44
Frieland (English frigate), 89
Friso (John William, 'Prince of Orange'), 22
Fürstenwaerther (Charles-Léopold, Colonel in RSR), 106

G

Gadebusch (battle of), 24
Gallenberg (Monsieur de, Second Captain in RSR), 106
Gálvez (Bernardo of), 85
Gardie (Magnus Julius, Count of, officer in RSR then general), 18
Gardie (Ulrich Gustaf, Count of), 35
Gardiners Islands, 71
Gartman (Axel), 89
Gates (Horatio, American general), 88
Gatines (Monsieur de, officer, French regiment of Lyonnais), 97
Gedda (officer in RSR), 106
Geffroy (Auguste), 69
Geijer (Erik Gustaf), 9
Georgetown (Port-Mahon, Minorca), 91
Germans (soldiers who form the RSR), 3, 4, 9, 35, 43, 46
German Brigade (French brigade including Germans), 3
German (French royal regiment), 107

Gérone (Siege of, Catalonia), 10, 11
Ghent, 20, 35
Gibraltar (siege of), 1, 2, 90, 91, 92, 93, 95, 96, 98, 99, 100
Gilles (Jean, French composer), 14
Glorious Revolution, 3
Gloucester (River and town, New South Wales), 79, 80, 81
Gooke (Lieutenant-colonel in Sparre regiment), 19
Göttingen (Deutschland), 36
Gouvion (Jean-Baptiste), 72
Grasse (François Joseph Paul, Count of), 76, 77, 78, 79, 83
Great Britain (Britain, England), 5, 14, 15, 23, 29, 32, 39, 44, 67, 84, 88, 89, 109
Great Northern War, 16, 24, 25
Great Winter, 20
Grenada, 88
Gribeauval (Jean-Baptiste Vaquette de), 43, 45
Gribeauval (type of canon), 80
Grönhagen (Johan Vilhelm, Sieur de, Major of the RSR), 44
Guadeloupe, 83
Guard (the Old), 43
Guibert (Jacques-Antoine-Hippolyte, Count of), 26, 45
Guichen (Luc Urbain du Bouëxic, Count of), 82, 90
Guinier (Arnaud), 45
Gustaf I Vasa (Eriksson, King of Sweden), 29
Gustaf II Adolph (King of Sweden, nicknamed 'the lion of the north'), 1
Gustaf III (King of Sweden), 31, 46, 68, 87, 88, 101, 105, 106, 107

H

Habsburg (Sovereign house of), 1, 14, 25, 27, 29, 30, 39
Haendel (Georg-Friedrich), 32
Hague (treaty of), 26

Hamilton (Hugo, Count of), 68, 92
Hanover, 32, 39, 40, 41
Hård (Erik, Second Lieutenant in Sparre Regiment), 13
Hartford (Connecticut), 72, 85
Hastenbeck (battle of, Deutschland), 40
Hay (Lord Charles, Major general), 29
Head-of-Elk-River (Chesapeake bay), 78
Henry (Cape, Virginia), 83
Henry IV (de Bourbon, King of France), 11
Hesse-Darmstadt (Georg of), 12
Hessian (mercenaries), 67
Holker (John, Junior), 69
Holm (Peter), 89
Holy Roman Empire, 1, 2, 3, 5, 14, 16, 20, 23, 24, 25, 30
Holstein (Erik Magnus Staël von, Baron of), 46
Hook (Nathanael of, 'Baron Hooke of Hooke Castle'), 16
Hopken (officer in RSR), 106
Hospitalet (battle of, Catalonia), 13
Hostalric (Siege of, Catalonia), 9, 11, 12
Howe (Richard, English admiral), 95, 98
Hudson (river), 77, 84
Hulst (siege of, United Provinces), 16
Hungary, 3, 28, 30
Hussars (French elite light cavalry including Hungarian), 3, 31, 73, 89
Huy (Belgium), 34

I

India (Indians), 39, 71
Innocent XII (Pope), 14
Invincible (The, French flagship), 100
Irish Brigade (French brigade, the 'Guard'), 107
Italy, 19, 26, 27

J

Jamaica, 83, 85
James II Stuart (King of England, Irland and Scotland), 3, 13, 15
James III Stuart, 15
Jarnac (dragons of, French cavalry regiment), 36
Jean-Baptiste (the, French ship), 92
Jeanne-Jacob (the, French ship), 92
Johnson (Charles, pirate captain), 89
Johnson (Amandus), 88
Jomini (Antoine Henri, baron of), 105, 106
Jones (John Paul), 90
Joseph I (Holy Roman Emperor), 25

K

Karl XII (King of Sweden, 'Iron Head'), 16, 20, 25
Kassel (Deutschland), 41
Kermina (Françoise), 101, 109
Kibling (Second-Lieutenant in Sparre Regiment), 17
Kings Ferry (Florida), 77
Klie (Monsieur de, officer, French regiment of Bouillon), 97
Klinckowström (Rudolf Maurits), 69, 70, 78
Knorring (Frans von, captain in Leisler Regiment), 6, 9, 11
Knorring (French regiment of), 13
Koblenz, 43, 107
Krefeld (battle of, Deutschland), 41

L

Lafayette (Gilbert du Motier, Marquis of), 68, 72, 76, 78
La Hay (The Hague), 34
Lameth (Charles-Malo of, French general), 69
Landau (Deutschland), 25
Landrécies (France), 24, 103
Lanière (forest of, Belgium), 21
Lauffeld (battle of, Belgium), 35
Lauter (River), 19, 32
Lauzun (Armand Louis de Gontaut, Duke of), 70, 72, 73, 78, 81, 83, 86, 88, 89
Lauzun (Légion of, Cavalry), 70, 75, 77, 103
Legislative Assembly, 109
Leisler (Johan Henrik, Captain), 6, 7, 9, 11
Lenck (Jakob Gustaf von, officer in Sparre Regiment, Colonel, Marshal,), 18, 19, 23, 25, 28
Leopold I (Holy Roman Emperor), 5, 14
Lesouef (Pierre), 81
Leuthen (battle of, Poland), 40
Leuze-en-Hainaut (battle of, Belgium), 9
Lewenhaupt (Adam Ludwig, Count of), 5, 6
Liège (French royal regiment of), 108
Liewen (Otto Heinrich, Baron of), 32
Lilliehöök (Captain then Colonel in RSR), 34
Lindbergh (Gunnar Wilhelm), 13
Lobkowitz (Johann Georg Christian von, Prince, Feld-Marshal), 30, 31
Longwy (France), 27, 108
Lorraine (Camille de, Prince of), 42
Lorraine, 27
Louis (Fort), 44
Louis (Saint, quay of, Strasbourg), 36
Louis (Saint, Order of), 37
Louis of France (son of Louis XIV, 'le Grand Dauphin'), 14
Louis of France ('Duke of Burgundy'), 15, 21
Louis XIV (King of France), 3, 5, 6, 10, 13, 14, 15, 16, 19, 20, 22, 23, 24, 25
Louis XV (King of France), 25, 26, 27, 28, 30, 31, 33, 37, 40, 41
Louis XVI (King of France), 42, 46, 69, 88, 90, 92, 95, 105, 106, 107, 109

Louisiana, 39
Louvois (François Michel le Tellier, Marquis de), 40
Lutterberg (battle of, Deutschland), 41
Lützen (battle of, Deutschland), 1
Luxembourg (François-Henri de Montmorency-Luxembourg, French Marshal), 6, 9, 10
Luynes (Charles-Philippe d'Albert, Duke of), 28, 33
Luzerne (César Henri Guillaume of the, Baron of Chambon), 71, 82, 83, 84
Lynch (Isidore of), 1
Lyonnais (French regiment of), 91, 92, 93, 95, 97, 100

M

Maastricht (siege of), 35
Madin (Henry, French composer), 33
Madrid, 87
Maës (Michel de, Major of the RSR), 44
Mahón (Fort, siege of, Minorca), 40, 91, 92, 93, 95, 97
Maillebois (Jean-Baptiste Desmarest, Marquis de, French Marshal), 30
Maintenon (François d'Aubigné, Madame de), 19
Malaga, 93
Malesherbes (Chrétien Guillaume de Lamoignon de), 42
Malplaquet (battle of, Belgium), 16, 21, 22, 24
Mannerheim (Second Lieutenant in RSR), 43
Marie-Antoinette (Queen of France), 46, 72, 85, 87
Mark (French regiment of the), 44
Marlborough (John Churchill, Ist Duke of), 17, 18, 19, 20, 21, 23
Maria-Theresa (Queen of France), 14
Maria-Theresa (Habsburg Empress), 39

Mary II (Queen of England, Scotland and Ireland), 12
Matthies (Christian, Sergeant in RSR), 110
Maubeuge, 22, 103
Maugras (Gaston), 72, 81
Maximilian Henry of Bavaria (Archbishop of Cologne), 5
Mayer (Antoine, Sergeant, French regiment of Bouillon), 100
Mediterranean, 90, 91, 92
Médoc-Infanterie (French regiment), 69
Meijer (Johan), 90
Meisenheim (castle of, Deutschland), 28
Menin (Belgium), 19
Mercy-Argenteau (Florimond, Count of), 69
Mésange (street of, Strasbourg), 36
Mesquida (bay of, Majorque), 91
Meuse (River and valley, France, Belgium), 110
Michaud d'Arçon (Jean, Chevalier de, French general), 1, 2, 90, 92, 93, 95, 96, 97, 98, 99
Minorca (siege of), 90, 91, 92
Montfort (Jean Bulot de, Sub-lieutenant of the fusiliers in RSR), 97
Montaigne (Monsieur de, Second Captain in RSR), 97
Montbarrey (Alexandre Marie Léonor de Saint-Mauris, Prince of), 43, 68
Montpellier (France), 68
Moonlight (battle of the, Cape St-Vincent battle), 90
Mons (Belgium), 6, 19, 21, 34
Moselle (French Army of the), 17, 107
Most Holy Trinity (the, Spanish flagship), 90
Murray (James, English general, governor), 91, 96

Myring (Baron of, Lieutenant in RSR), 97

N

Namur (Belgium), 19, 34
Nancy (France), 27
Nantes (Edict of), 5
Napoléon, I 76, 80, 81
Nardin (Pierre), 45
Nassau-Siegen (Charles Henri Nicolas Othon, Prince of), 97, 98, 99
Nassau (French regiment of), 44, 97, 98, 99
National Assembly, 107
National Convention, 109
National Guard (French revolutionary regiment), 108
Navarre (French regiment of), 26
Necker (Suzanne, born Curchod), 46
Necker (Jacques), 68
Neerwinden (battle of, Belgium), 10
Nelson (Horatio), 90
Netherlands, 5, 6, 14, 15, 34, 109
Neustadt-am-Rübenberge (Deutschland), 40
New England, 77
New York, 67, 71, 72, 73, 74, 75, 76, 77, 79, 84, 85
Nijmegen (battle of), 15
Nine Years War, 5, 13
Nioldarm (Monsieur de, Captain Commanding in RSR), 97
Noailles (Anne-Jules, Duke of, French marshal), 9, 10, 11
Noailles (Louis Marie Antoine, Viscount of), 72
Noailles (Louis, Duke de, Marshal of France), 32
Noël (Mathieu, Sergeant, known as 'mouchi', french regiment Bretagne), 100
Nordenskiöld (Otto Henrik), 87
North (French Army of the), 107, 108, 110

North Carolina, 74
Nuremberg, 20
Nystad (Treaty of, Finland), 2
Nyvenheim (Walther von, Colonel in RSR), 101

O

O'Connel (Daniel Charles, Count of), 97, 99, 100, 107
O'Hara (Charles, English general), 80, 81
Orfèvres (street of the, Strasbourg), 36
Orléans (Philippe, Duke of), 19, 25, 26
Ormond (Duke of), 23
Orrery (English brigade of), 21
Ottoman Empire, 28
Oudenarde (battle of, Belgium), 20
Oxhufvud (Swedish captain in Sparre Regiment), 12

P

Palamos (siege of, Catalonia), 11, 12
Palmqvist (Magnus Daniel), 87
Panissars (Pass of, Catalonia), 9
Paris, 2, 4, 6, 7, 10, 13, 16, 19, 20, 21, 23, 26, 28, 29, 30, 31, 33, 44, 46, 69, 71, 72, 82, 90, 92, 102, 105, 106, 107, 108, 109
Paris (treaty of), 101
Pastora (the, French pram), 98
Paulette (the, French corvette), 91
Pèlerin (the, French ship), 92
Pensacola (siege of), 87, 88
Peter of Russia ('the Great'), 2, 3, 16, 20, 24
Pettersèn (Adolph Fredrik, 'Rosenvärd'), 88
Pfaffenhoffen (battle of, Deutschland), 33
Pfennings (tower, Strasbourg), 36
Phalsbourg (France), 36
Philadelphia, 67, 69, 77, 82, 83, 84, 85, 86, 88, 89

Philip IV of Spain (King of Spain), 14
Philip V of Spain (King of Spain), 20, 25, 26
Philippeville (Belgium), 101
Philipsburg (siege of, Deutschland), 27, 28, 77
Picquet de la Motte (Tousaint-Guillaume, 'La motte-Picquet'), 100
Piper (Carl Fredrik), 44
Poiret (Grenadier Lieutenant in RSR), 32
Poland, 16, 24, 27, 71
Polignac (Gabrielle, Duchess of), 69
Polish (French royal regiment), 43
Polish Succession (war of), 27, 28
Poltava (battle of, Ukraine), 20
Pompadour (Jeanne-Antoinette Poisson, Marquise of), 40
Pont (Jacob Wilhelm de), 70, 85, 89
Ponceau (Doigny du), 42
Portelance (Philippe), 30
Port-Mahon (Minorca), 91
Porto-Cabello (Venezuela), 87
Portsmouth (New Hampshire), 83
Portugal, 5, 15, 90
Potomac (river), 78
Pradon (François, Sergeant, French regiment of Lyonnais), 100
Pragmatic Sanction, 24, 29
Prague, 30, 32
Princeton (battle of), 67
Protestants, 1, 2, 5, 13
Providence (port of), 77, 85
Prudhomme (Louis-Marie), 108
Prussia, 4, 15, 27, 29, 30, 32, 39, 40, 43, 96, 106, 108
Pulaski (Kazimierz, Count of), 88
Puységur (Jacques François de Chastenet de, Marquis, Marshal of France), 22, 26
Puységur (Louis Pierre de Chastenet, Count of), 45

Q

Queffen (Monsieur de, Sub-Lieutenant of the Chasseurs in RSR), 97
Quesnoy (Le), 22, 24
Quiévrain (Belgium), 108
Quincy (Charles Sevin, Chevalier de), 21

R

Raab (Carl), 87
Rakoczi (Francis II, Prince of Transylvania), 3
Ramillies (battle of), 19
Ranger (American frigate), 90
Rastatt (treaty of), 25
Reasonable (English ship), 89
Reutersverd (Officer in RSR), 106
Rhineland, 16, 18, 27
Rhine (River), 16, 20, 32, 33, 39, 41, 106
Rhode Island, 70, 71, 85
Richelieu (Louis-François-Armand de Vignerot du Plessis, Duke of), 40
Rochambeau (Jean-Baptiste-Donatien de Vimeur, Count of), 68, 69, 70, 72, 73, 74, 75, 76, 77, 78, 79, 81, 83, 84, 85, 86, 87, 107
Roch (Saint, France), 68, 96
Rocourt (battle of, Belgium), 34
Rodney (George Brydges, Baron of, Admiral), 72
Rohan (Louis-René, Cardinal, Prince of), 28
Rohan-Soubise (Charles, Duke of, Marshal of France), 41
Rosas (Siege of, Catalonia), 7, 8
Rousseau (Monsieur de, Second Lieutenant of the Grenadiers in RSR), 97
Royal-Allemand (French regiment), 3
Royal-Corsican (French regiment), 3
Royal Italian Regiment (French regiment), 3

Royal-Louis (the, French flagship), 92
Royal Swedish regiment (French regiment known as 'Royal Suédois'), 1, 3
Ruremonde (siege of, Netherlands), 16
Russia, 2, 16, 20, 24, 27, 29
Russia (Anna of), 24
Ryswick (treaty of, Netherlands), 13

S

Sackville (John, Lord), 36
Sahay (battle of, Bohemia), 30
Saint-Domingue (Haïti), 14, 76, 77
Saintes (battle of the, Dominica), 83, 85
Saintonge (French regiment of), 70
Saint-Tropez (the, French ship), 92
Saint-Germain (Claude-Louis, Count of), 40, 42, 43
Saint-Philippe (fort of, Minorca), 2, 93
Saint-Simon (Louis de Rouvroy, Duke of), 19
Salis (French regiment of), 36
Sambre-et-Meuse (French regiment of), 110
Sandershausen (Deutschland), 41
San-Roque (Spain), 93, 94, 96, 101
Saratoga (battle of), 67
Sardinia, 27
Sars (forest of, Belgium), 22
Sarsfield (Patrick, Count, 1st Earl Lucan), 10
Savannah (State of Georgia), 87, 88
Savoy (Duchy of), 5, 15
Savoy (Victor-Amadeus, Duke of), 12, 15
Savoy-Carignan (Eugène of), 22
Saxe (François Xavier, Prince de, Count of Lusace), 24, 31, 34, 36, 40
Saxony (Maurice de, Marshal of France), 23, 24, 30, 33, 34, 36

Saxony (Frederich-August I, King of), 24, 27
Scheffer (Per, Captain in RSR), 33, 37, 39
Scheffer (Ulrich, Lieutenant in RSR), 33, 34, 35
Schellenberg (battle of, Deutschland), 33
Schiomaire (Calld 'the Elder', Sub-Lieutenant in RSR), 103
Scottish Guard (personal guard of the kings of France), 3
Schulenburg (Marshal von der), 24
Sébastian (Saint, Spain), 26
Ségur (Pierre, Marquis de), 12
Ségur (Philippe-Henri, Marquis de, French Marshal), 33, 70, 92
Sereau (Raymond), 90, 97, 98, 99, 100
Sérieux (the, French ship), 92
Serruriers (street of, Strasbourg), 36
Seven Years War, 1, 39, 42, 44
Sierck (Moselle), 18
Silesia, 32, 39
Sintclair (Carl Gideon, Major of the RSR), 41
Sisce (Jean-Baptiste de Bressoles de, Sub-Lieutenant, French regiment of Bretagne), 97
Soissonnais (French regiment of), 70
South Carolina, 81
Spa (Belgium), 106
Spain, 5, 12, 14, 15, 23, 25, 26, 27, 90, 91, 92, 96
Spanish Succession (war of), 15, 90
Sparfelt (Lieutenant-colonel), 6
Sparre (Erik Magnus, Major von Fürstenberg, Count of Sunday, Baron de), 11, 12, 13, 15, 16, 18, 19, 20, 22, 24
Sparre (French regiment of, commanded by Eryk Magnus Sparre), 11, 19, 21, 22
Sparre (Karl Magnus de Toffeta, Baron of), 12, 25, 26

Sparre (Joseph Magnus de Toffeta, Count of, son of Karl Magnus), 25, 26, 30, 33, 35, 36, 37
Sparre (Louis-Ernest, brother of Joseph Magnus), 15, 44
Sparre (Lars Magnus, cousin of Karl Magnus), 12, 20, 27
Sparre (Alexander, Count of, son of Joseph Magnus), 37, 39, 42, 43, 45, 106
Sparre (Axel Gabrielson, Second Lieutenant in Sparre Regiment), 12
Sparre (Ernest Louis Joseph, Count of), 45, 95, 101, 102
Sparre (Charlotte Frédérica, 'Lotta'), 102
Spartel (Cape of, Marocco), 100
Sprengtporten (Göran Magnus, Colonel), 45
Stanislas I (Leszcynski, King of Poland), 27
Stedingk (Curt von, Count of), 45, 46, 68, 87, 88, 103
Steenkerque (battle of, Belgium), 9
Steward (House of), 83
Stierneman (Olof von), 33, 45
Stockholm, 6, 28
Stollhofen (Deutschland), 20
Strasbourg, 28, 36
Stuppa-Jeune (Swiss regiment in the service of France), 6, 7
Stützer (Captain in Sparre regiment), 19
Sullivan (Eleanore), 109
Sultana (the, French ship), 91
Sundahl (Christian, Captain), 89
Sweden, 1, 2, 3, 4, 5, 9, 11, 13, 16, 17, 19, 20, 24, 25, 28, 31, 33, 34, 35, 39, 44, 45, 46, 68, 88, 89, 101, 102, 103, 105, 106, 107
Swiss (Royal Guards of the French Crown), 3, 6, 11, 30, 107, 108, 109
Sweden (Adolf Fredrik, King of), 34

T

Talla-Piedra (French pram), 97, 98, 99
Taube (Bernt Wilhelm von, captain in Leisler Regiment), 9, 11, 13
Te Deum, 6, 14, 28, 32, 33, 40
Tellier (Louis Charles César, Duke of Estrées, Marshal of France), 40
Ter (River, Catalonia), 8
Ternay (Charles-Henri-Louis d'Arsac, 'Knight of'), 70, 72
Terror (reign of the), 2
Tessin (Carl Gustaf, Count of), 28
Thirty Years War, 1, 2, 3
Thomas (Jean-Pierre), 41
Thomas (Saint, church, Strasbourg), 36
Thorn (siege of, Poland), 16
Tideman (Lieutenant in RSR), 43
Tongres (Belgium), 35
Tortola (Don), 91
Torwigge (Nils Vilhelm, Baron of), 35
Toulon (France), 81, 91
Tour (Monsieur de la, officer, French regiment of Bouillon), 97
Tournai (Belgium), 16, 17, 21, 25
Touzot (Jean), 46
Trarback (siege of, Deutschland), 27
Trenton (battle of), 67
Trier (siege of), 18, 27
Tuileries (Palace of the, Paris), 107, 109
Turgot (Anne Robert Jacques, Baron), 42
Turin (treaty of), 12
Two-Bridges (French regiment of), 44, 70, 85
Two-Esters (American frigate), 89

U

Uggla (Georg Gustaf), 88
Ulfsparre (Åke, af Browvik, Captain in Leisler Regiment), 9, 11, 12

Ulfsparre (Edvard, captain in Royal Swedish Regiment), 43
United Provinces, 5, 7, 90
United States, 67, 68, 70, 78, 87
Upham (Charles Wentworth), 78
Uppsala, 89
Urgel (siege of, Catalonia), 9
Ushant (battle of, France), 82
Utrecht (treaty of), 20, 23, 24

V

Valenciennes (France), 103, 105, 108
Valmy (battle of, France), 109
Varennes (France), 105, 109
Vaudreuil (Louis-Philippe, Marquis of), 85
Vaux (Noël Jourda, Count of, Marshal of France), 68
Velasco (Fernandez de, 8th Duke of Frías), 13
Vendôme (Louis-Joseph de Bourbon, Duc de), 11, 12, 13, 19, 20
Verberie (France), 45
Villars (Claude-Louis-Hector de, Marshal of France), 16, 17, 18, 19, 20, 21, 22, 23, 24, 25, 27, 28
Vintimille du Luc (Charles Gaspard Guillaume de, Archbishop of Paris), 33
Vergennes (Charles Gravier, Count of), 68, 70, 92
Vernier (Jules), 31
Versailles, 28, 29, 32, 33, 40, 68, 73, 87, 101, 103, 105, 109
Ville de Paris (French flagship), 79
Villeroy (François de Neufville de, Marshal of France), 18, 19
Vioménil (Charles du Houx, Baron of), 77
Vioménil (Antoine Charles du Houx, Baron of), 77
Virginia, 74, 76, 77, 78, 82, 83
Voltaire (François-Marie Arouet, Writer, philosopher), 16, 23, 27, 30

W

Waldeck (Georg Friedrich, Prince von), 6
Washington (George), 67, 70, 71, 72, 74, 75, 76, 77, 78, 79, 81, 83, 84, 87, 88, 103
White Haven (raid of), 89
William and Mary (College, Virginia), 78
William III of Orange, 13
Williamsburg (Virginia), 78, 79, 82, 83
Wilmington (Delaware), 86
Wissembourg (Deutschland), 32
Wodnian (castle of, Bohemia), 30
Wrangel (Fredrik Ulrik, historian), 7
Wrede (Ferdinand Josef, Baron then Prince of), 35

Y

Yorktown, 77, 78, 79, 81, 84, 87, 89
York (river, Virginia), 79

www.ingramcontent.com/pod-product-compliance
Lightning Source LLC
Chambersburg PA
CBHW070555170426
43201CB00012B/1847